The 15-Second Handstand

A Beginner's Guide

by Chris Salvato

Copyright © 2013 Chris Salvato

All rights reserved No part of this publication may be reproduced, stored in a retrieval system or transmitted in a form by means, electronic, mechanical, photocopied, recorded, or otherwise without the poor written consent of the publisher. The authors and publisher disclaim any responsibility for any adverse effects or consequences from the misapplication or injudicious use of the information presented in this text.

Swift Archer LLC
500 North Rainbow Boulevard
Suite 300A
Las Vegas, NV 89107
USA

Dedicated to Serena who encouraged me to finish each page, to my enthusiastic readers who showed me I had knowledge worth sharing, and to my teachers, to whom I owe everything.

Disclaimer

By using The 15-Second Handstand: A Beginner's Guide and any of its promotional or video content (hereafter as referred to the "Book"), you (hereafter referred to as the "User") signify your agreement to these Terms and Conditions. If you do not agree to all of these Terms and Conditions of use, do not use the Book!

The use of the Book and suggested workouts, exercise routines, nutritional suggestions, or other suggestions is <u>at your own risk</u>. In no event shall the Book, its authors, editors, illustrators, its suppliers, or any third parties mentioned in the Book be liable for any damages in the future including, but not limited to, heart attacks, muscle strains, pulls or tears, neck, back, shoulder, elbow, wrist, hand, finger and/or hip injuries, and other illness/disease, or injury/damage (mental, physical, financial), however caused, occurring during or after altering any personal nutritional, fitness, lifestyle habits or actions. The Book and author do not assume any responsibility for any aspect of healthcare administered with the aid of content available in the book. User understands that any and all advice/programs concerning exercise is not done under supervision of a qualified trainer and nutrition is for educational purposes only. User has been advised to seek medical advice from a physician before altering their nutritional daily diet or beginning an exercise program.

Foreword

I have been performing handstands for years and teaching anyone who wanted to listen everything that I have learned along the way. When I wrote a short article on my blog (http://www.chrissalvato.com) about handstands, I was floored with the response. The internet and book shelves across the globe are rife with materials about the handstand and hand balancing. There is an overabundance of information available. So why are so many people interested in what I had to say?

In the 20th century, the western world had lost sight of the effectiveness of simply moving our bodies through space. A vast majority of gyms are filled with machinery meant to work muscles, but not bodies. Fitness and health, like so many other parts of our lives, has turned into a grind. The gym is seen as another horrible necessity if we want to avoid the tyranny of disease, ugliness and untimely death. How very grim. The fitness world has swung into habits to avoid despair.

These sorts of trends, however, come full circle. Nature has a way of correcting itself, and I believe that fitness trends are moving in the right direction. We are moving toward enjoying our workouts and their results. As more people learn to master their own bodies, the fitness industry moves inches in a better direction. Conquering your body and the physical world is impressive and rewarding. As you do so, the monotony of moving weights attached to strings and pulleys loses its appeal.

No feeling is quite as rewarding as the mastery of moving yourself through space – whether running, jumping, climbing or hand balancing. Rewarding still is your new abilities unlocking a whole new world before you. Runners often experience this after their first effortless mile, craving to run their first 5k, then their first marathon. Similarly, the handstand unlocks an array of advanced and impressive feats of strength and skill. It shatters the monotonous world of treadmills and Smith machines, making it nearly impossible to go back. And yet, many with interest struggle to get started.

When I first learned to handstand, it took me over one year to get my first 15-second freestanding hold. It took me that long to put together all of the pieces of the puzzle and learn what worked. I developed an addiction to handstands. I was obsessed with getting it right. But one year is far too long and I eventually was able to get others to their first handstand in a fraction of the time.

My goal in writing this book is to provide accessible information and insight about the handstand so that you, or anyone else, can attain your first handstand in weeks, not years. My intended audience are complete beginners, not those with years of hand balance training. Beginners need a program they can start today without minutiae and details.

This book lays out a minimalistic program that will enable you to perform your first handstand. Perfect form is not the goal for a beginner, and not the goal of this book. As a beginner, your goal is to stand on your hands, and my goal is to get you there.

Over the better part of a decade, I have refined this material to enable newcomers to get their first 15-second freestanding handstand within as little at 40 days. My program attacks the difficulties in learning the handstand as an adult, and boils it down into the simplest possible steps. The rest of this book explains why these methods work so well, and will broaden your understanding as you tackle advanced (and impressive) handstand and bodyweight skills training.

WAIT! Before you start...	**10**
Get Started. Right Now.	**12**
Two Step Method	13
28-day Commitment Log	*15*
Evaluate Your Current Ability	*19*
Challenge 1: 60-Sec Wall Plank	21
Challenge 2: 60-Sec Wall Handstand	28
Challenge 3: First Pirouette Bail	37
Challenge 4: The 4-Points Checklist	49
Challenge 5: Backward/Forward Control	62
Challenge 6: The HDLU Kick-up	70
Handstands, Strength and Skills	**78**
Why the Handstand	79
Strength vs. Skill	80
Adult Handstand Difficulties	84
The Psychology of Progress	**89**
Conquering Fear	90

The Physics of Balance   94

How Balance Works   96

Translating Basic Physics To The Body   98

Cambered Hand Technique   102
Optimizing Body Position   106
Advanced Body Position Discussion   120

Losing Control of Balance   140

The Physiology of Posture   149

The Brain's Understanding   150

Teaching Your Primitive Brain   153

Physiologically Preparing for Handstands   162

Dynamic Control: The Kickup   169

Beyond Your First Hold   174

Appendix   177

Pre-Challenge 1: Downward Dog   178

WAIT! Before you start...

Did you know that you also receive special *bonus content* that is available only to readers of this book? By buying this book, you actually purchased much more than a physical book; you get tons of bonus resources, also!

To claim your bonus content, sign up at and receive access to articles and tools including:

- **Commitment Tracker** - Keep yourself on track!

- **Sport Integration** - Wondering how to integrate CrossFit and handstands? Or how to integrate handstands with yoga? The bonus resources explains how.

- **Overcoming Obstacles** - Address the most common handstand challenges...and how to overcome them.

- **Beyond 15-Second Handstands** - What to do once you hit this goal, including the elusive One-Armed Handstand.

- **Case Studies** - Learn from the mistakes of others!

Claim Your Premium Bonus Content
http://chrissalvato.com/bonus-content

Thousands of my handstand students prefer to learn through video. If you're interested in video demonstrations of *each* step in the progression, then visit my website to make your purchase and *speed up your progress immediately.*

> **Special:** *46% off videos for readers of this book!*
> http://chrissalvato.com/private-video-offer

Get Started. Right Now.

Most people can get to their first 60-second handstand against the wall within 28 days and their first freestanding handstand within 60 days. In fact, you are probably a lot farther along than you think.

You are reading right now because you want to learn handstands, so why wait until you are done with this book to get started? Instead, start right now. There is no reason to delay. It doesn't really matter how old, weak, frail or clumsy you are – start right now. Once you start executing the steps in this program, the details in the rest of the book will be in much better context.

Two Step Method

The handstand isn't really that hard. It seems difficult to you because your brain has been programmed your whole life to stand on your feet and stay upright. As a result, most of the problems with learning the handstand are not with your body. *They're with your brain.* The good news is that we can get past that.

Part of the problem is fear, and part of it is a loss of the ability to balance on anything aside from your feet. Surprisingly, holding a handstand doesn't take much physical strength. (OK, if you want to hold one for 5 minutes, you are going to need to be pretty conditioned. To get your first impressive 15-second or even 1-minute hold, it really doesn't take so much strength.) Getting your first handstand takes only two things: *conquering fear* and *consistent practice*.

Despite popular belief, perfect form is not necessary. There is no need to get bogged down with unnecessary steps just so that you can have "perfect" form. Perfect is the enemy of good. Instead, you need to focus on the few key actions that will have the biggest impact on progress, rather than harping on small imperfections that won't move you closer to your goal. To get started immediately and stay on the right track, you only need to take two steps:

1. Start using a 28-day Commitment Log
2. Evaluate your current ability

28-day Commitment Log

Commitment and consistency with a training program is the most challenging and most influential component to success. Your success relies heavily on keeping a small log of your activity. Here is how it works:

1. Create a spreadsheet similar to Figure 1
2. Every day, do at least 5 minutes of handstand work
3. When you finish, you put an "X" in that day's box

START DATE	7/1/13
Day	5 minutes of handstands today?
7/1/13	X
7/2/13	X
7/3/13	X
7/4/13	X
7/5/13	X
7/6/13	X
7/7/13	X
7/8/13	X
7/9/13	
7/10/13	
7/11/13	
7/12/13	
7/13/13	
7/14/13	
7/15/13	
7/16/13	
7/17/13	
7/18/13	
7/19/13	
7/20/13	
7/21/13	
7/22/13	
7/23/13	
7/24/13	
7/25/13	
7/26/13	
7/27/13	
7/28/13	

Figure 1: Example 28-day Commitment Log

Checking off the boxes in your log, however, isn't just to record your progress. It's a goal - a challenge. Every day, find some time in the day to set a 5-minute timer. Most smart phones have a timer built in or, you can use http://e.ggtimer.com/5minutes. Anyone, no matter the circumstances, can manage 5-minutes of handstand training for the day. If you are too tired to train on some days, you can even sit and meditate about handstands for 5-minutes. You just want to get into the habit of having handstands be an integral part of your life.

To create this level of consistency, you can latch your training to an *anchor event*. An anchor event is an event that *must happen* in your daily routine. Something like having breakfast, waking up, or going to bed. For example, you may practice handstands every day before breakfast; maybe every day after getting home from work; maybe every day after dinner; or maybe you work on your handstands as the last thing in the day, just so that you get it done. Put a reminder near something related to the action event - like a sticky note on your refrigerator, headboard or bathroom mirror so that you remember to do your workout at the time you planned. Again, don't worry about working the whole 5 minutes, but just set aside 5 minutes every day. The goal is to make handstand practice a habit. The limiting factor in the handstand is not building strength, but staying consistent.

The "Never Two In A Row" Rule

The handstand spreadsheet is incredibly helpful when building a commitment. It's amazing how satisfying it can be to put that big red "X" onto your spreadsheet. But life creeps up even on the best of us. Maybe you needed to rush your child to the doctor, and spent the day in the hospital. Maybe some friends invited you on an all day hiking trip, and before you knew it you were exhausted, enjoying a drink by the campfire at 1:00 AM. Sometimes we are just forced to take a day off for one reason or another.

When that happens, don't beat yourself up. Missing training days like this is a fact of life. It happens even to professional athletes. It's easy to fall out of the habit before it even starts because you accidentally missed a day during the challenge. Subconsciously, you already count yourself as a failure, just because you missed one day!

The best way to handle these small missteps is to employ the "Never Two In A Row" rule to systematically tackle this problem. When you absolutely, positively *must* miss a day in your handstand training, put a red "O" into the spreadsheet or on your calendar. The goal is to never have *two* "O"'s together, and to keep them to an absolute minimum.

Employing this method will help keep you consistent, because then a single missed day won't be such a huge failure. Instead, its just a small bump in the road that you hit before moving on to success.

Evaluate Your Current Ability

The 15-Second Handstand (15SH) progression consists of six major milestones. The first two can usually be completed within the first 28 days. All six have taken as little at 40 days, but may take a few months depending on your unique situation. The milestones include:

1. 60-Second Inclined Wall Plank
2. 60-Second Wall Handstand
3. First successful pirouette bail
4. Fixing form (with the 4-Points Checklist)
5. 10-second handstand near a wall, but without touching
6. Kicking up into a freestanding handstand

To evaluate your current ability, try to perform the lowest level skill (60-Second Inclined Wall Plank). If you succeed, try to perform the next skill (60-Second Wall Handstand), and so on. The following sections outline the instructions for each of these milestones, including a daily workout and step-by-step actions you need to take to progress to the next milestone. You should always be working towards the next skill in the progression. Once you achieve a milestone, immediately progress on to the next one.

Challenge 1: 60-Sec Wall Plank

Goals:
1. Build pre-requisite arm strength
2. Get used to being inverted

This skill is a safe way to start learning your limits on the handstand. First, place your hands on the floor and assume a normal push-up position. Then, walk your legs up the wall so that your feet are just slightly over your head as shown in with a straight body (no saggy hips!). Acceptable positions are shown in Figure 2. This is the position to hold. Once you can hold this position for 60 seconds, you are able to progress to the 60-Second Wall Handstand.

Figure 2: Acceptable Wall Plank Positions

Daily Routine For This Challenge

5 minutes of wall plank practice every day, aiming for a full 60-second hold. The timer starts when your elbows are locked. The easiest way to spend your 5 minutes is to perform a maximal hold each time. This works well for people with a solid fitness background.

If you are just starting to get into upper body strength work, then you may have more success by testing your max hold once every other day, or even once a week. If you take this approach, then all of your other holds should be 50% to 75% of your max. For example, if your max is 45 seconds, your holds aside from the max can be 30 seconds.

Many newcomers find that daily physical training will be too taxing for this challenge. In many cases, you may prefer to take every other day off. For this challenge (and Challenge #2), that is perfectly acceptable. However, when you are not physically training, you should spend 5 minutes sitting in a quiet space with your eyes closed, visualizing perfect handstand form. Visualize your body becoming longer and stretched out into a perfectly balanced handstand.

If you do this for 5-minutes on your "rest days," you have satisfied your training quota. This will greatly help with your physical training[1], will provide adequate recovery while you build the pre-requisite strength *and* will keep your daily streak going.

Whichever approach you take, make sure you take 1 minute of rest between attempts, and try to walk your hands closer to the wall each time, until you are about 12 inches from the wall, and feel completely safe.

At no point should you feel that you are in danger of falling over yourself. You should also stop your workout if you get fatigued to the point where you are unsure that you can support your weight.

Extra Credit - Beyond the Daily Routine

This section is for people who want to work on their handstands for more than 5 minutes per day. Since this challenge is only difficult for those who need to build a foundation of strength, it is important to not overwork yourself, so training more than a single 5 minute session should be done cautiously.

If you really feel that you can be doing more, I don't want to hold you back, though! You can do multiple 5-minute sessions per day, but limit each session to 3 holds, with 1 minute rest in between. Don't exceed 10 holds in a single day, as rest and recovery are crucial to progress in strength training. In other words, adding in extra wall plank holds will likely be counter productive at this point.

Finer Points

The purpose of this position is to get you used to being inverted, and takes your first steps towards the end goal. This position isn't that much different from a normal pushup position, so it should be relatively easy to get over the fear and see immediate progress.

The main goal is to get addicted and over fear, so don't analyze your form too much. At this stage, the only key point on form is to keep your elbows locked. The timer starts when they are locked and ends when you break straight elbows. Don't worry about any other details about your form just yet. At this point, everything else doesn't matter as much. You can look like a complete mess, so long as your elbows are locked and hips aren't sagging. In the simplest terms, you are just trying to get your hips over your head.

If you have a fitness background, you might blast right through this part of the progression, but it is an important test to perform. If you are a complete newcomer, then this is where most people in your position need to start.

Questions and Answers

Q: This is too hard! What can I do to work up to this?

If this is too hard, you can work up to the inclined plank using the Downward Dog yoga position. This move is covered in the [Appendix](#).

Q: My feet are slipping down the wall! What do I do?

There's a few options here. If you don't care about the wall, just wear rubber soled shoes (sneakers/trainers) to get more traction. You can also put your feet on a chair or other elevated surface that you can move up over time. As you walk you handstand towards the wall, you can also bend at the hip, as shown in the middle frame of [Figure 2.](#) This will stop your feet from sliding down as you lean your weight on the ball of the foot.

Q: My head feels like it's going to explode! How can I avoid this?

Increased pressure is a common sensation for people who are not used to being inverted. If, however, you are experiencing *pain* then **stop the workout immediately** - especially if you notice your eyes going bloodshot. You should check with your doctor, as extreme pain is normally a sign of high blood pressure and, in rare cases, can cause blood to pool in the eyes.

For those people cleared by their doctors, most issues arise from your body not knowing how to cope with being upside down yet, so you need to teach it. To get over this, simply keep practicing and remind yourself to breathe. Bring your feet up as much as you can, and when your head starts to hurt, take the pressure off by lowering your feet a little. This normally goes away within the first 7 days of consistent training, though it can take up to 14 days, and can sometimes take 6 weeks or more.

Q: Holding this position is causing wrist pain. What do I do?

You are suffering from a severe lack of mobility in the wrists. I would recommend getting parallettes or pushup trainers to start, while working on wrist mobility at the same time. An example of acceptable pushup trainers can be found here: http://amzn.to/12AkUWm. This equipment will take the pressure off of your wrists at this early stage. If you don't want to invest in equipment, a later part of the 15SH progression includes the Cambered Hand Technique, which takes a lot of strain off the wrists. You may want to jump ahead in the progression to learn this hand position. For severely limiting pain, you may need to look into wrist mobility techniques and stretches as perscribed by a doctor/physical therapist. Once you're cleared by a doctor, you can attempt to perform wrist flexibility/strengthening techniques as described in this article: http://chrissalvato.com/2013/11/handstand-wrist-pain/. Focusing on wrist mobility will slow down your progress on the handstand but will contribute to better overall joint health.

Q: Where am I supposed to be looking? What is the right head position?

At this point, just find a comfortable posture. The proper head position is between your arms, looking at your hands, but head position isn't critical at the moment.

Q: Should my hips be sagging?

If you haven't caught on by now, your hips should not be sagging! Fix sagging hips by bending at the hip, thinking about creating an L-shape with your body as shown in Figure 2. Your form doesn't need to be perfect but sagging hips put a lot of strain on the lower back. You don't need to create a complete L-shape, but erring towards an L-shape is much better than saggy hips, which results in a C-shape.

Challenge 2: 60-Sec Wall Handstand

Goals:
1. Continue building arm strength
2. Get completely inverted
3. Confront fears

Now we slowly progress toward a full inversion. First, place your hands on the floor and assume a normal push-up position. Then, walk your legs up the wall so that your feet are completely over your head. Figure 3 shows how to achieve this position, with the ultimate goal being a chest to wall handstand. You don't need to hit this exact form just yet – your hands can be farther away from the wall if that is easier for you and your form doesn't need to be as rigid. Figure 4 shows another version of less desirable (but perfectly acceptable) form for this stage of the progression. The only requirement, and most crucial part of this progression, is making sure that your elbows are locked.

Figure 3: Achieving ideal wall handstand form

Figure 4: Achieving acceptable wall handstand form (not ideal, but OK)

Daily Routine For This Challenge

Five minutes of wall handstand practice per day building up to a 60-second wall handstand hold. The 60-second timer starts when your elbows are locked, and the rest of your form doesn't matter.

Similar to Challenge #1, people with a solid fitness background find it easiest to spend your 5 minutes is to perform a maximal hold each time.

People who are new to upper body strength work, however, may have more success by testing your max hold once every other day, or even once a week. If you take this approach, then all of your other holds should be 50% to 75% of your max. For example, if your max is 45 seconds, your holds aside from the max can be 30 seconds.

Many newcomers find that daily physical training will be too taxing for this challenge. In many cases, you may prefer to take every other day off. For this challenge (and Challenge #1), that is perfectly acceptable. However, when you are not physically training, you should spend 5 minutes sitting in a quiet space with your eyes closed, visualizing perfect handstand form. Visualize your body becoming longer and stretched out into a perfectly balanced handstand. This will greatly help with your physical training[1], will provide adequate recovery while you build the pre-requisite strength *and* will keep your daily streak.

Whichever approach you take, make sure to rest for about 1 minute of rest between attempts, and stay about 12 inches from the wall. You should feel completely safe; you should not feel in danger of falling over.

You should walk out of the handstand, so make sure you have enough strength to walk out of each attempt. This means walking out at the first sign of fatigue or shaking.

This challenge is the slowest one for most people who need to build strength, but slow and steady will win the race here. Stick with it, because the rest of the challenges are much easier by comparison.

Extra Credit - Beyond the Daily Routine

This section is for people who want to work on their handstands for more than 5 minutes per day. Similar to Challenge #1, this challenge is only difficult for those who need to build a foundation of strength. It is important to not overwork yourself, so training more than a single 5 minute session should be done cautiously.

If you really feel that you can be doing more, I don't want to hold you back. You can do multiple 5-minute sessions per day, but limit each session to 3 holds, with 1 minute rest in between. Don't exceed 10 holds in a single day, as rest and recovery are crucial to progress in strength training. In other words, adding in extra wall plank holds will likely be counter productive at this point.

Another way to train more would be to jump ahead to Challenge #3, and start practicing pirouette bails. To avoid fatigue, only hold the handstand for a second or two when you train pirouette bails...but don't jump too far ahead! It will be overwhelming!

You want to hit the 60-second wall handstand benchmark before moving on to Challenge #4, but attempting a few pirouettes every day will speed up the progression, over all.

Finer Points

Don't worry about being perfectly straight, pointing your toes, keeping your legs straight or even being close to the wall when first starting. You will get used to being upside down. Most of the adult population will never achieve this position and if this is the first time, congratulations! You should hold onto this feeling and let it empower you through the rest of this program. Now the handstand is actually within reach.

Commonly, achieving your first 60-second hold with locked elbows will take 7 to 14 days when starting to work on this position. Don't be discouraged, however, if it takes just a bit longer. The only real metric is holding the position a little bit longer each day - even if the difference from one day to the next is under a second.

If you have crippling fear about bringing your hands closer to the wall, then *don't do it*. Once you can hold a reasonably inverted 60-second hold, with your hands 12 inches from the wall or less (like the one in Figure 4), then you can move onto the Pirouette Bail – this is your weapon to cut down fear. The next step in the progression (learning the Pirouette Bail technique) will reduce anxiety about bringing your hands closer to the wall, which is important for working towards a freestanding handstand hold.

Questions and Answers

Q: I am too scared to get close to the wall. What do I do?

Walk your hands closer to the wall until you are comfortable with your position. Do not go beyond your comfort zone just yet. Once you can hold the most inverted position possible for 60-seconds, while not being scared, you can progress onto the handstand pirouette bail. Ideally, you want your hands to be under 12 inches from the wall before progressing.

Q: I am not perfectly straight against the wall. Is this OK?

At this point, being perfectly straight isn't necessary. The most important thing is maintaining locked elbows. Your back can be a little arched, and your legs can be all wonky – that doesn't matter right now. Just get inverted and keep those elbows locked!

Q: I don't know how to lock my elbows. How can I get them locked?

Imagine you are pushing hard into the ground. Imagine you are pushing the entire Earth away from your body – as far away as it can go. Assuming you are strong enough, this should straighten the elbows, and ideally cause your shoulders to push towards your ears.

Q: I can't achieve a "hollow body position." What should I do to fix this?

I haven't addressed the "hollow body position" yet, but many people have this question at this stage, probably because of how much it is used in handstand information all over the Internet. While the hollow body position is important to some of handstands, it is not important for our purposes at the moment, so don't worry about it yet.

Q: My head feels like it's going to explode! How can I avoid this?

As stated in the previous section, this is a common sensation for people who are not used to being inverted.

A sensation of increased pressure is common. As with any workout, if you find yourself in *pain* then **stop the workout immediately**. This is especially true if you notice your eyes going bloodshot. Extreme pain is normally a sign of high blood pressure and, in rare cases, can cause blood to pool in the eyes. Definitely check with your doctor if any of these issues arise for you.

To reiterate from Challenge #1, your body simply doesn't know how to cope with being upside down yet. To get over this, simply keep practicing and remind yourself to breathe. Bring your feet up as much as you can, but when your head starts to hurt, take the pressure off by lowering your feet a little. This normally goes away within the first 7 days of consistent training, though it can take up to 14 days and can sometimes take 6 weeks or more.

Q: Holding this position is causing wrist pain. What do I do?

I mentioned this in the previous section, but if you are starting with Challenge #2, and skipped Challenge #1, then you should be aware of it.

As stated in the previous section, you are suffering from a severe lack of mobility in the wrists. I would recommend getting parallettes or pushup trainers to start, while working on wrist mobility at the same time. An example of acceptable pushup trainers can be found here: http://amzn.to/12AkUWm. This equipment will take the pressure off of your wrists at this early stage. If you don't want to invest in equipment, a later part of the 15SH progression includes the Cambered Hand Technique, which takes a lot of strain off the wrists. You may want to jump ahead in the progression to learn this hand position. For severely limiting pain, you may need to look into wrist mobility techniques and stretches as perscribed by a doctor/physical therapist. Once you're cleared by a doctor, you can attempt to perform wrist flexibility/strengthening techniques as described in this article: http://chrissalvato.com/2013/11/handstand-wrist-pain/. Focusing on wrist mobility will slow down your progress on the handstand but will contribute to better overall joint health.

Challenge 3: First Pirouette Bail

Goals:
1. Learn bailing technique
2. Completely conquer fear

Once you get used to being inverted, it is time to conquer the fear that is inhibiting your freestanding handstand. To do so, you need to learn how to bail out of the handstand. As you get more comfortable being inverted this nagging fear of falling head-over-heels onto your back needs to be eliminated. The pirouette bail is the safest, easiest and most versatile of the bailing techniques. It takes only a minute or two to learn in person. It is not very intuitive or easy to explain to a beginner through the written word, so an in-depth explanation is necessary.

Daily Routine For This Challenge

Five minutes of pirouette bail practice with a minimum of 5 attempts per day. For every 3-5 attempts that you make without rest, you should be resting for about 1 minute. This ensures that you are not getting fatigued, and can learn this skill effectively.

Extra Credit - Beyond the Daily Routine

This section is for people who want to work on their handstands for more than 5 minutes per day. Since this challenge is the first *skill* that you will be working on, you can train it as much as you like through the day. The more you practice, the faster you will progress.

You can practice more often by performing multiple 5-minute sessions every day, or doing one-off pirouette attempts throughout the day. Since this skill only requires that you have an open wall with some free space, it can be done anywhere throughout the day.

Finer Points

A full handstand pirouette is simply a 90 degree turn, sometimes called a quarter turn. That's all. The Pirouette Bail, though, is a partial turn (not necessarily a full 90 degree turn), that is used to move your body forward *just enough* to let your legs come down safely. In essence, don't go trying to "perfect" this move into a full quarter turn. That is not the goal here.

It's easiest to learn the skill when we break it down into the five distinct parts. The images in Figure 5 show each of these steps occurring. It happens fast in real-time, so these steps are not immediately obvious.

1. You are in a good handstand.
2. You start to overbalance. Overbalancing is losing balance towards your back, where you are going to go head over heels.
3. All of your weight is shifted to a single arm, the planted arm.
4. The leg and shoulder opposite to the planted arm is pushed forward, turning your body.
5. You bring your feet down, safely bailing.
6.

Figure 5: The Pirouette Bail - Step-by-Step

Note that, when learning, you need to force yourself to overbalance in Step 2. When first learning, many people try to shift their weight to the planted arm and rotate without overbalancing. This *will not work*. It will cause your feet to come down too fast or your wrists to twist unnaturally. Instead, focus on purposefully overbalancing.

Notice that the planted arm and leg stay in a straight line, in step 4. The leg and hips opposite to the planted arm goes forward just a little bit. This causes the body to turn. By shifting all of your weight to a single arm, you create a pivot point. Then, by shifting the opposing leg forward, you are creating torque around that point.

In a full pirouette, you turn the whole 90 degrees, but since this is a bail, you are just trying to move your free arm forward as much as necessary to let your legs come down safely. If that means you come all the way around in a complete quarter turn (90 degrees), that's fine. If you only move your hands a little bit, but your legs come down safely, that is good, too.

The bail is not a full pirouette; it is a means of getting your hand slightly in front of you so that you can come down safely.

Figure 6: Different pirouette bail hand placements

Practicing Techniques

This challenge is a bit different to the previous challenges, in that there are a few options in how you can practice. Feel free to mix and match any of the methods below as you experiment with them. These options are listed out in order of my personal preference.

A. Wall Pirouettes

This progression is the most direct, and most familiar since it utilizes the wall just like the previous progressions for your 60-second wall handstand. The steps can be cued "*Shift-Push-Lower*" as follows:

1. Go into your best handstand against the wall.
2. **Shift** all of your weight to one arm, the planted arm. Don't hold this too long as it will take a lot of strength. Go into step 3 ASAP.
3. **Push** the opposing leg, hip or shoulder out, leaning your weight over the body. *Purposefully overbalance.* This causes your body to start turning, and overbalancing is crucial. Many people find that driving the *opposite* toe into the wall mitigates the fear when starting to overbalance.
4. **Lower** your legs to the ground (this should happen automatically).

Figure 7: The Wall Pirouette Bail - Step-by-Step

Don't try and hold step two for very long. This would be the equivalent of one-armed handstand training, which is too difficult for a beginner. Instead, shift your weight quickly and push your opposing leg, hip or shoulder out. If this works for you, congratulations! You just got the handstand pirouette bail in a few minutes, something that literally took me 6 months to figure out on my own.

This is usually the most direct route for people who are already pretty strong in overhead pressing and support, but the nature of shifting the weight slowly may be difficult for those with less experience.

B. Wall Corner Pirouettes

If you are a bit anxious getting started, then you can use two walls to build up to the Wall Pirouettes progression. This progression is the same as the Wall Pirouettes progression, but you perform the move in the corner of a room to provide a second wall onto which you can lean.

1. Go into your best handstand against the wall.
2. **Shift** all of your weight to one arm, the planted arm. Don't hold this too long as it will take a lot of strength. Go into step 3 ASAP.
3. **Push** the opposing leg, hip or shoulder out. This will cause your body to start turning. *Purposefully overbalance.* Your body will start turning, and overbalancing is crucial. Many people find that driving the *opposite* toe into the wall mitigates the fear when starting to overbalance.
4. Turn until all of your weight rests on the second wall.
5. **Lower** your legs to the ground (this should happen automatically).

Figure 8: The Wall Corner Pirouette Bail - Step-by-Step

C. Spotted Pirouette Bails

For those still struggling, you may need to seek out a spotter to help you. If you need to use a spotter, this indicates that your handstand progression will take slightly longer for you since you will have to do quite a bit more fear conditioning.

Using a spotter works much better if you are a relatively small person, which is why it is used heavily in children's progressions. As an adult, using a spotter requires a high level of trust in the person who is spotting you. Even with a great spotter, there is usually some fear or anxiety (on both ends) about kicking the spotter in the face. It does work for a lot of people, though.

The spotter stands off to the side with one arm straight out to provide support. You kick up, avoid kicking them in the face, and they hold both of your legs, supporting your weight. It may take a few tries just to get used to this position, spotter and hand balancer alike.

To practice pirouettes, the spotter removes their grasp from one of your legs and you *purposefully overbalance* and shift your weight to the planted arm. The planted arm, in this case, is on the same side that the leg is holding. As you overbalance, you should naturally rotate enough to come down.

Questions and Answers

Q: I am not sure I am doing this right...how do I know when I have done this successfully?

If you can overbalance and get your feet to the ground, you are doing this properly. If you are not doing this properly, then you will not be able to overbalance and save yourself. Of course, that means that you do not need to do a full 90-degree quarter turn. The goal of this is to avoid falling head-over-heels from overbalancing. If you can do that, you can bail safely - which is the whole point of this milestone.

Q: I'm not strong enough to shift my weight. What do I do?

You are taking too long to push your opposite leg, hip or shoulder forward, which is turning a quick shifting of the weight into a one-armed handstand hold. The weight shifting should be done quickly, and just enough to lift your other arm off the ground.

Q: I just can't get this skill. It's frustrating! Can I move on anyway?

Yes, you can move on, but you won't get far. Fear is the biggest obstacle of handstand progress for adults. By ignoring your fears, you are just delaying your plateau even further.

One effective way to get over this fear is to seek out an open gym in your area. Most places (even small towns in the US and Europe) have a local gymnastics facility or leisure center that has an open gym training period. These sessions usually cost $10-$20 USD (£6-£12 GBP; €8-€16), and allow you to surround yourself with mats and foam to help you if you fall over. There are usually other gymnasts and instructors at these sessions, as well, who may be able to provide a spot.

After you purposely fail a few times in the safe environment like an open gym, you may be surprised at just how little it hurts, which can work wonders in conquering your fear and learning the skill. (Do keep in mind that you fall and fail at your own risk, just in case you weren't paying attention to the disclaimer at the beginning of the book.)

While my progressions work for most people, if you find yourself still struggling then you may want to work on another pirouette bailing technique like the handstand roll bail. The rolling bail is covered in Jim Bathurst's tutorial on handstands, found at the Beast Skills website: http://www.beastskills.com/the-handstand/

The handstand rolling bail is not covered in this book because the rolling bail is more difficult, more technical and very limiting. In other words, it's not well aligned with your immediate goals. Only the pirouette can be done safely on any surface; rolls need to be done on a soft, even surface. Learning to pirouette bail, is the only way to truly conquer your fear.

Challenge 4: The 4-Points Checklist

Goals:

1. Improve form

2. A 60-Second Wall handstand using 4-Points Checklist

Now that you can pirouette, you should have no fear about getting very close to the wall – close enough for the chest to touch. Similar to your 60-second wall handstand hold, you will walk up the wall into full handstand position. The difference, however, is that you will focus on the major form fixes that you cannot fix when you are afraid of falling head-over-heels. These form fixes better prepare you for freestanding holds. They will also make holding your wall handstands much easier, since you will learn to rely on good biomechanics, rather than brute strength.

Daily Routine For This Challenge

At least 5-minutes of wall handstand work focusing on the 4-Points Checklist. Similar to Challenge #1 and #2, the easiest way to spend your 5 minutes is to perform a maximal hold each time. This works well for many people, but some people still find this approach too taxing.

If this is too taxing for you, then test your max hold once every other day, or even once a week. If you take this approach, then all of your other holds should be 50% to 75% of your max. For example, if your max is 45 seconds, your holds aside from the max can be 30 seconds.

Whichever approach you take, make sure to rest for about 1 minute of rest between attempts. At no point should you feel that you are in danger because the pirouette bail can save you. You should stop your workout if you get fatigued to the point where you are unsure that you can support your weight.

Extra Credit - Beyond the Daily Routine

This section is for people who want to work on their handstands for more than 5 minutes per day. Since this challenge is heavily strength-based, performing extra holds every day may be counter productive. Instead, you can continue to practice wall pirouette bails (while keeping in mind the 4-Points Checklist) throughout the day. This will ensure that you are as comfortable as possible with bailing, since it is absolutely crucial for success in Challenge #5 and #6.

Finer Points

Fixing major form flaws will make supporting your body easier. At this stage, most people will suffer from at least one of the following form flaws:

1. **Soft Arms** – Elbows are not locked out
2. **Sagging Shoulders** – Shoulders are not active
3. **Splayed/Wonky Legs** – Spread or haphazard legs
4. **Soft Legs** – Knees, ankles and/or hips are not rigid

You may not suffer from all of these, but it is worthwhile to learn the cues (small visualization tricks) that help you fix these problems and achieve better form.

(Note that none of these flaws have anything to do with banana-back or hollow-body as you may see in a lot of other handstand progressions. While hollow-body is a better position for progressing onto skills like the one armed handstand, the banana-back form is perfectly valid for standard handstand holds. Whichever form you learn first will be easier, and the other will be harder to learn, but this is not a problem. After all, your goal is to get a freestanding handstand so there is no need to be picky when you can just set a week aside to learn the hollow body position later on.)

The Cues

1. Each of the following cues on the 4-Points Checklist will help fix at least one major form problem. Step through each of the cues in turn, and keep them in mind whenever you are inverted. At this beginning stage, work on only ONE of these at a time to avoid getting overwhelmed.

4-Points Checklist

1. Push hard into the ground
2. Shrug your shoulders to your ears
3. Lock your knees together
4. Reach for the sky

Push Hard Into the Ground

By pushing hard into the ground, you force your body to straighten the elbows by *pushing hard into the ground*, thus fixing Soft Arms, which is the most important form flaw of all. Aside from thinking to "push hard", it can help to go overboard and visualize that you are pushing the entire earth away from you. As shown in Figure 9, you may also experience the benefit of having your shoulders shrug up to their ears by using this cue.

FRONT SIDE

**NO LOCKED ELBOWS
NO ACTIVE SHOULDER**

**LOCKED ELBOWS
NO ACTIVE SHOULDER**

**LOCKED ELBOWS
ACTIVE SHOULDER**

Figure 9: Visualization of the *push hard into the ground* cue

Shrug Your Shoulders To Your Ears

Shrugging your shoulders to your ears is worth mentioning this all on its own because it plays a crucial role to handstand support. This fixes the Sagging Shoulders form flaw by forcing an the Active Shoulder position shown in Figure 10, which is a common hand balancing and lifting position that increases shoulder stability and control.

FRONT   SIDE

NO ACTIVE SHOULDER

ACTIVE SHOULDER

Figure 10: Visualization of the *shrug your shoulders to your ears* cue

Lock Your Knees Together

Once your shoulders and elbows are locked, you need to make sure that your lower body is aligned properly by *locking your knees together*. Obviously, fixing Splayed/Wonky Legs will help with total body alignment. While pushing hard into the ground, and shrugging your shoulders, focus on bringing your knees together. This helps distribute your weight evenly on both hands, and thus make balancing in the handstand easier. Some forms of the handstand make use of the straddled position, with legs spread apart, but having your knees locked together better promotes a rigid body which is easier for balancing. Thus, locking your knees together as shown in Figure 11 is very helpful the beginner with their sights on their first hold.

Figure 11: Visualization of *lock your knees together* cue

Reach For the Sky

Finally, while pushing hard into the ground, shrugging your shoulders, and locking your knees together, *reach for the sky*. Feel your body elongate, your spine straightening as your toes reach upward. You should notice your glutes and hamstrings (butt and back of the legs) tightening, helping to keep your entire body rigid and aligned. This cue will fix soft legs, as the hip, knees and ankles all get fully engaged when you try to reach for the sky. By making the body as long and tall as possible, it is easier to get the body directly over the hands in an optimal balancing position. It also engages the spine, which reduces the strain on load bearing joints and musculature, which helps to increase hold duration. When you are against the wall, your toes may not be pointed - that's ok. When you start to work on this cue when freestanding, though, you will find that your toes naturally find a pointed position.

Figure 12: Visualization of the *reach for the sky* cue

Do It Yourself

Now that you know the key flaws, and the cues that counter them, get against the wall and practice. Every time you get into a handstand against the wall, walk your hands as close to the wall as possible. By now, that should mean your hands are only a few inches from the wall.

First focus on *pushing hard into the ground,* move on to *shrug your shoulders,* then *lock your knees together* and finally *reach for the sky.* You want to get into a habit of running through the 4-Point Checklist every time you are in the handstand position. Many people are able to nail down the 4-Points Checklist and achieve a 60-second hold within 7-10 days of starting this challenge - but everyone progresses at their own pace.

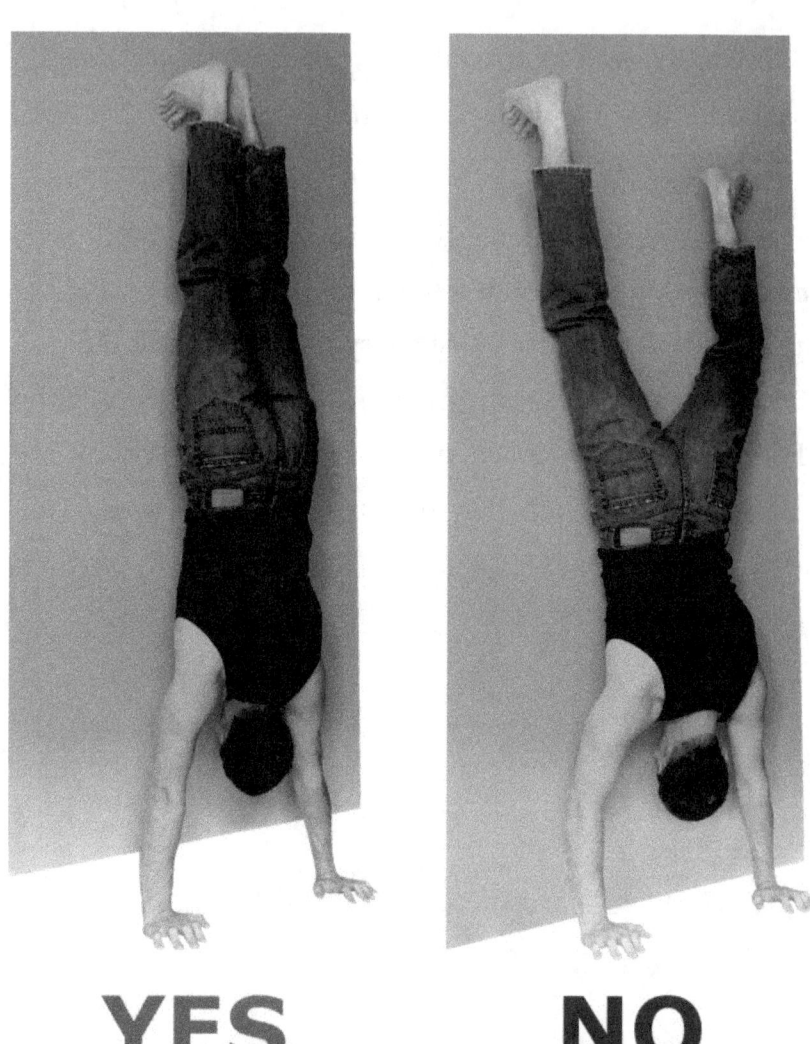

Figure 13: Illustration of acceptable vs. poor wall handstand form

Questions and Answers

Q: My wrists hurt, am I doing something wrong?

No, but if you struggle from wrist mobility problems, you may feel some discomfort on the longer holds. You can alleviate this problem by jumping to the next section to learn about the Cambered Hand Technique. When reading about the technique, apply the hand position but don't worry about forward-backward control just yet.

Q: I am scared to get too close to the wall, which is making it hard to Reach For The Sky. What can I do?

You need to remember that you know how to bail and save yourself. Walk your hands closer to the wall, and if you start to fall forward, pirouette bail to safety. If you find that this is still scary for you, practice your pirouette bails every day until you find that fear waning, then try this progression again.

Q: Can I skip this step? I can already hold myself up for 60-Seconds.

If you look like the photo labelled "No" in Figure 13, then no, you should not skip this step and focus on a 60-second hold with the form fixes from the 4-Point Checklist.

Challenge 5: Backward/Forward Control

Goals:
1. Gain control of balance
2. A 10-sec handstand near the wall, but without touching

Your fears of falling over should be remedied (or at least lessened) by the fact that you have a weapon against them - the pirouette bail. You now need to work on a single key element that gives you control of your balance - the Cambered Hand Technique.

Daily Routine For This Challenge

5 minutes of wall handstand practice per day, attempting to hold a handstand for 10-seconds near the wall, but without touching. Pull one leg away from the wall, and position it over your head, shoulders and hands. Tap the other foot away gently and hold as long as possible. This will train you to balance using the cambered hand technique. Pirouette to safety if you overbalance.

Repeat this process as much as possible within your 5-minute session, but rest for 30-60 minute every 1-5 attempts. If an attempt was very taxing (for example, a total hold of 30+ seconds), then you should rest after that single attempt.

If you bail quickly after each attempt, you should rest after the fifth to recuperate.

Extra Credit - Beyond the Daily Routine

This section is for people who want to work on their handstands for more than 5 minutes per day. Since this challenge is heavily skill-based, you want to train near-the-wall balance as much as possible. This means that you can do multiple 5-minute sessions every day, or make one-off attempts at near-the-wall balance as much as possible throughout the day. The more the better (so long as you aren't overly fatiguing yourself)!

Finer Points

The cambered hand technique makes balancing easier in nearly all hand balancing skills. This includes the planche, frog stands, L-sit, V-sit, handstand presses and much more. The easiest way to get into a cambered hand position is to place your hand flat on the floor, then curl your fingers up into the proper position. Lean your weight into your hands slowly, as shown in Figure 14. Get a feel for the hand position, and how it differs from the flat-handed position.

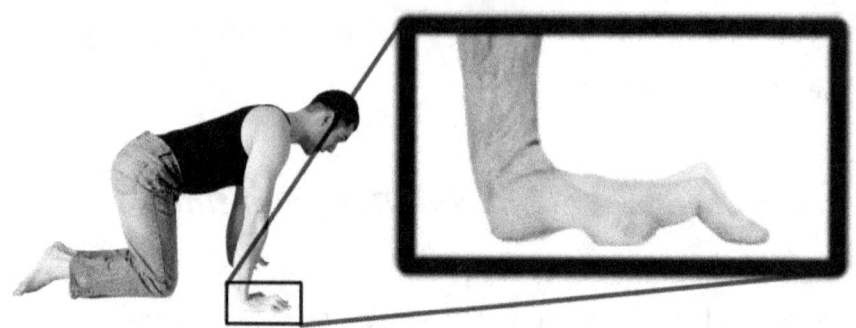

Figure 14: Close up view of Cambered Hand Technique

If you still don't understand how to achieve this position, consider the following mini-progression shown in <u>Figure 16-1</u>, <u>Figure 16-2</u> and <u>Figure 16-3</u>:

1. Place hands together in front of you
2. Keep palms and thumbs touching and pull your fingers apart
3. Touch the tips of your fingers together, while keeping the long part of the digits from touching

Figure 16-1: Step 1 - Place Hands Together

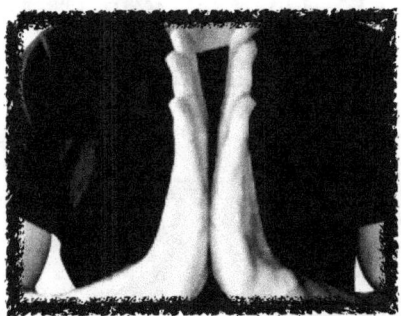

Figure 16-2: Step 2 - Keep palms and thumbs touching. Pull fingers apart.

Figure 16-3: Step 3 - Touch the tips of your fingers together.

The cambered hand position is the perfect example of a small change that has a huge effect on your handstands. It provides two solid points of contact with the ground - your palm, and your fingertips. Conceptually, you can assign a role to each point of contact:

1. When you are underbalancing (falling towards your stomach), *push* into your palms.
2. When you are overbalancing (falling towards your back), *push* or *grip* with your fingertips.

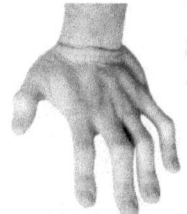 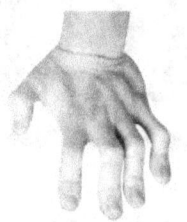 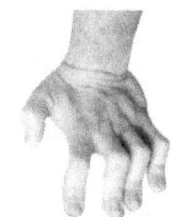

UNDERBALANCED   BALANCED   OVERBALANCED

Figure 17: Comparison of hands in different states of balance. Notice the *grip* is more pronounced as you approach being overbalanced.

When using the Cambered Hand Technique, the fingers are no longer fully extended, so the forearm muscles are no longer fully stretched. This means that your wrist flexors are now in a more advantageous position to grip the ground and influence your balance

Do It Yourself

Now that you know the secret of the cambered hand technique, try it for yourself:

1. Walk into a handstand against the wall
2. Pull your fingers into a cambered hand position
3. Pull one foot over your head, shoulders and hands
4. Tap the other foot away from the wall, so you move into a freestanding handstand
5. Grip hard with your fingers to pull yourself back

It will take a bit of practice to get the feel for it. Experiment by moving your toes off of the wall and gripping hard to force your body back against the wall. Another effective method of practicing this is to perform your handstand in a narrow hallway. Sway back and forth in the hallway by purposefully pushing the palms into the floor and catching yourself on the opposing wall. Then, grip hard into the floor to drive your toes back into a wall handstand.

Once you are able to take your toes off of the wall and balance yourself for a few seconds, you have reached another milestone. Continue to practice this to master freestanding balance. Within a week, you should feel that you have better control your balance by squeezing your fingers and relaxing your grip. It is just a matter of time (and practice) before you can use this newfound ability to hold a freestanding handstand near the wall for 10 seconds or more.

Questions and Answers

Q: I have been using parallettes instead of flat hands. Does this apply?

Yes. If you have been using parallettes because of wrist pain, then try the cambered hand technique as it may alleviate your wrist pain in normal handstands. You may not need the parallettes anymore (though they are very useful for training handstands with a different grip). If you want to continue using parallettes, then you will abduct your wrists when you underbalance, and adduct your wrists when you overbalance as shown in Figure 18.

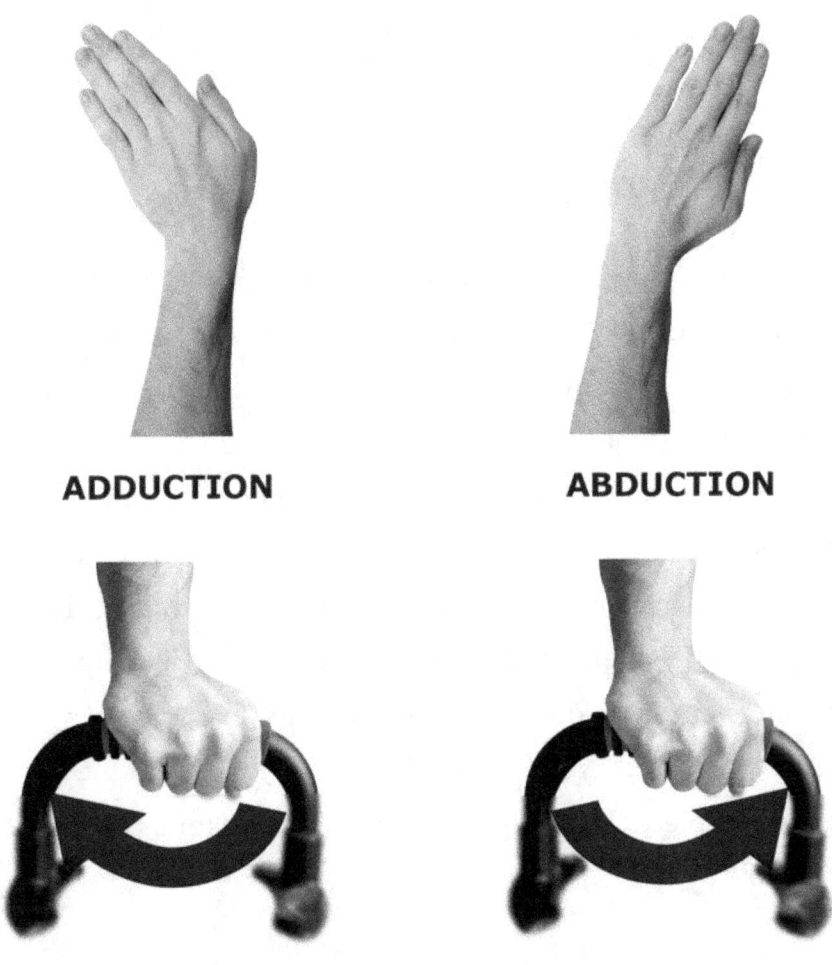

Figure 18: Wrist adduction and abduction

Q: Will this work even if my form isn't perfect?

Yes. The only requirement is that your elbows are completely locked out. If the elbows are not locked out, you cannot transfer force down to the rest of the body efficiently and it won't be nearly as effective.

Challenge 6: The HDLU Kick-up

Goals:
1. Learn to Kick Up

With a firm grasp on all previous challenges, the only remaining component to learn is a safe kick-up technique for your first freestanding holds, free of all walls and safety nets. At this stage, you should be able to hold a 60-90+ second handstand against the wall, be comfortable with your Pirouette Bail and have started to feel yourself gain control in your balance using the Cambered Hand Technique. That means that you are ready to start practicing the kick up, and taking control of your balance from there. Once you can gain control after your initial kick-up, you put all of the previous pieces together to maintain balance for as long as possible.

Daily Routine For This Challenge

At least 5 minutes of handstand work a day, performing at least 5 kickup attempts, based on your skill level (Wall HDLU, Freestanding HDLU, Freestanding Kickup). Hold the resulting handstand as long as possible, using the Pirouette Bail when overbalancing (if freestanding).

If your kickup attempts fail immediately, then you can kick up again immediately. Limit immediate-retries to 5 times, then take a 30- to 60-second rest. Rest for at least 10-30 seconds after successful kickup attempts (2+ second holds) to allow yourself to regroup.

Extra Credit - Beyond the Daily Routine

This section is for people who want to work on their handstands for more than 5 minutes per day. Since this challenge is heavily skill-based, you want to train your handstand kickup as much as possible. This means that you can do multiple 5-minute sessions every day, or make one-off attempts as much as possible throughout the day. The more the better (so long as you aren't overly fatiguing yourself)!

Finer Points

The kick up is one of the most difficult things to learn on your own and will likely be one of the most valuable part of this book for you. The 15SH progression in this book uses the HDLU Technique to gradually learn the components of a successful kickup.

The HDLU Technique

The HDLU in HDLU Technique stands for Hands Down; Leg Up. To execute an HDLU, follow these steps:

1. **Hands Down** - Put your hands onto the floor with *cambered hands, locked elbows* and an *active shoulder*.
2. Lean all of your weight onto your hands.
3. Take *one leg* and stretch it as far back as you can.
4. **Leg Up** - Kick your straight leg up over your head *gently* and feel your other leg naturally lift off the floor. Note that the lift from the floor is passive. *This is not a jump.* Your leg should naturally come off the floor as your other leg goes up. Repeat this process, experimenting with a kick-up that is a *little bit* faster each time until you notice that you can hold yourself up for a second or two.
5. Squeeze into the ground to try and correct the overbalance and stand upright
6. Once your hips are over your head, bring your legs together so your ankles and knees are lined up

The HDLU progression starts against the wall, then moves onto a freestanding HDLU and ends, finally, with a freestanding kickup from the standing position.

Figure 19: The steps of the HDLU Technique (note that Step 5 is not shown because it is difficult to visually illustrate squeezing into the ground)

Do It Yourself
A. Wall HDLU

You get started with the HDLU by performing it against a wall. As you practice, you will gradually learn the right speed for your kick-up leg, using the wall to catch yourself when you over-estimate the force needed. Over time, you will find that you can hold yourself up, and extend your other leg.

This technique lets you get a feel for kick-up force easily and quickly. Since you can make several attempts in rapid succession, you will quickly learn the amount of force necessary for you to get your legs over your head. The wall removes the fear of falling, letting you focus entirely on the movement.

You can progress to Freestanding HDLUs once you feel that you can comfortably kick up into a balanced handstand for 1 to 3 seconds near the wall without touching it. This will help you learn the amount of force you need for the kick-up.

Figure 20: The Wall HDLU Technique

B. Freestanding HDLU

Once you are comfortable with the wall HDLU, remove the wall and focus on pirouetting out of bailed attempts. Do this until you can get a 1- to 3-second freestanding hold away from a wall.

Figure 21: The Freestanding HDLU Technique

C. Freestanding Kickup

With the Freestanding HDLU mastered, do the same, but start from standing. This isn't technically a gymnastics handstand kickup, but its close enough for a novice. It takes some work to minimize the force of the full kickup, but pirouettes will save you if you start to bail.

Figure 22: A freestanding kickup based on the HDLU Technique

Within a week, most people are able to hold a 1- to 3-second handstand from a Freestanding HDLU. Everyone progresses at a different rate, though. This is especially true of dynamic movements like the HDLU that require a lot of skill training. Within your first week of training this skill, shoot for at least a 1- to 3-second handstand from the Wall HDLU. Once you get a 1-3 second hold using the HDLU technique, you have successfully held your first freestanding handstand! Congratulations are in order.

Now that you can kick-up into a handstand, you may find that sometimes things will just "click" and you can hold your handstand for 5-10 seconds, but it will not be consistent. That means you are on the right track! Keep practicing and your hold times will be up to 10-15 seconds every time. The more frequently you train your handstand balance, the faster you will progress.

Questions and Answers

Q: I can kick up, but can't seem to hold it. What am I doing wrong?

You need to keep practicing – at least 5 minutes a day, but the more the better. Consistency is what got you this far, anyway, so just keep it up. If you are having a hard time progressing, think back to the 4-Points Checklist. Are you running through the 4-Points Checklist whenever you kick up?

If that alone does not help you, you may want to try scissoring the legs. This helps increase the stability of the hold, and is described in more detail in the section on <u>Advanced Body Position Discussion</u>.

Q: How can I get over the fear of doing my first Freestanding HDLU?

Are you as comfortable as you can be with the Pirouette Bail? Do you have any fear of falling head-over-heels? Practice light and gentle kick ups where there is no chance that you can fall head-over-heels. As you do so, Pirouette Bail immediately. Increase the power of your kickup on every attempt. Eventually you will see that you know how to save yourself every time.

Q: Where do I go from here?

Keep practicing until you can hold it for 10 seconds reliably, and then for 15 seconds. From there, you are among the ranks of hand balancers, and you can continue on to more advanced skills, like a 60-second hold, handstand pushups or handstand presses. There's more information on possibilities in the <u>last chapter</u> of this book.

Handstands, Strength and Skills

All of the previous sections of this book have covered the step-by-step progression to getting your first handstand. While this information is useful and valuable on its own, it is even more valuable to know how this progression works, and why it is so effective. After all, if you teach a man to fish, he will never starve, and knowing the underlying principles of this progression will help you apply the key elements to your other goals.

Why the Handstand

While the handstand is impressive and cool, it is hardly a mere parlor trick. If you are serious about dominating your own body to an impressive, awe inspiring level, then you simply cannot do so without mastering the handstand. No amount of barbell training can prepare you for the stresses of the handstand, and without the handstand, it is virtually impossible to progress to higher level bodyweight strength skills.

Handstands are a fundamental position in gymnastics and bodyweight strength. It is analogous to learning the chords in music or vocabulary in language. If you enter any gymnastics facility, you can ask every athlete in the building to perform the handstand. Those who perform the best handstands also perform better at everything else, just like the pianist who masters and practices their fundamental chords will undoubtedly be a better musician.

To be as effective as possible, I always look for the maximum output for minimal input. Life is short, after all, and there isn't time to be wasted in senseless, faulty progressions or lessons that do not produce results. Since the handstand is fundamental and has highest translation to all other skills, you will reap big rewards when you focus on the handstand in your training. Learning to handstand also unlocks an entire world of handstand skills unto itself. Handstand holds, handstand pushups, handstand presses, and one armed handstands simply cannot be attempted if you cannot perform a handstand. The handstand is a skill that should be trained every day if your goal is awe-inspiring mastery of your body.

Strength vs. Skill

For the completely uninitiated, bodyweight skills require two types of training - Strength and Skill. These two types of training are linked, but ultimately separate. In order to make optimal progress, it is important to understand the differences between them.

Strength training aims to make our bodies stronger and more capable to perform a specific movement or skill. If you are training your body to increase the amount of force you exert, then this is considered strength training. For example, you would increase the amount of force you exert in the squat by increasing the weight on your back. Strength training usually takes on the form of performing movements in sets and reps, or working to hold an isometric position longer. (Note that holding a position for 15-60 seconds is usually considered strength training, whereas holding a position for several minutes is considered *endurance training*.) Strength training sessions are usually relatively short, with long periods of rest, and usually require 1-3 rest days per week to generate optimal results.

Skill training is when a movement pattern is practiced through repetition and exposure to the skill. It is only through practice that any progress can be made in skill training. For a movement or exercise to be considered skill training means that you already posses the pre-requisite strength to perform the skill repeatedly without overexerting yourself. Skill training sessions are usually not very taxing but entail working at the skill for several minutes or hours at a time. Unlike strength training, you can perform skill training every day or even several times a day since the movements are not very taxing.

To better understand the relationship between skill training and strength training, consider a child learning to walk. The child needs to build up the necessary strength in their legs by lifting themselves up on the edge of a table or chair. At first, they are wobbly and weak, but over time they can stand with the support of a table for quite some time. Now that their legs are stronger, the child can move away from external support, and the skill training begins. When they first move away, they fall immediately. By exposing themselves to the skill over time, their brains and bodies get used to standing and walking. This usually results in a poorly made home video that is shared on YouTube or a Facebook feed.

Learning to perform a handstand is very similar to the progression a child moves through as they learn to walk. The handstand, then, is not purely strength based. Indeed, most of handstand training is in the realm of skill work. Of course, if you cannot hold yourself upside-down on your hands for more than a few seconds, you will need to build that strength. Once you posses the necessary strength, however, you must train the handstand as a skill (i.e., frequently). Handstand training sessions, then, gradually shift from a focus on sets of holds to a focus on practice and fixing form. The goal is to move into the realm of skill training as quickly as possible. You need get *addicted* to skill training so that you can invest dozens of hours a week with little effort.

Building the pre-requisite handstand strength can take less than 28 days if you invest at least 5 minutes per day. Once you have the pre-requisite strength, you can train handstand skills virtually anywhere. I have practiced my handstands in idle time at home, at work, at the park and just about everywhere else. When you get addicted, it's common to be training handstands for dozens of hours a week and not realize it. It is not far fetched to achieve your first handstand within weeks.

If getting addicted and investing dozens of hours a week into your handstand sounds overwhelming, don't worry. Firstly, the work is masked as an enjoyable break from the norm. Secondly, when getting started, a minimal investment of 5 minutes a day is all that is necessary. Even if you don't get addicted, 5 minutes per day is more than enough to make solid progress.

Adult Handstand Difficulties

Since there are so many free and disorganized handstand progressions on the internet, many adults waste years of reading and training without seeing any real results in their handstands. These faulty progressions are usually designed by those who teach children, or those who can perform the handstand and don't understand the challenges to an adult beginner. That is why my main claim in this book is going to sound foolhardy: **with consistent training, most adults can learn to hold their first freestanding handstand within 90 days.** This is not a bold claim, despite the difficulties you may have had with learning handstands. Sure, it may take a few people a bit longer than 90 days, but progress should always be measurable.

The first difficulty in learning the handstand is fear. The handstand strikes fear into the heart of most people over the age of 13. Something funny seems to happen between 9 and 13, where those who cannot do handstands suddenly feel condemned to a life without them. This is not without a good biological reasons. At about this age, your brain undergoes major physiological changes. In particular, the *pre-frontal cortex* and *amygdala* both change substantially - and both regulate fear.

The prefrontal cortex controls planning and mood modulation - it helps us make better judgements. The amygdala is a more primal part of our brain, that controls emotional reactions and anxiety. Somewhere during adolescence, these brain areas start to process our environment differently. The result is a more fearful view of the world. Things that used to be perceived as benign (like being held upside-down or doing a backflip) cause crippling fear.

This hit me hard when I was learning to do my first backflip at the age of twenty-three. Every time I attempted a flip, I needed to do a small meditation to force the fear out of my head. I would slap myself in the face to clear my mind before each flip. To my frustration, another man about the same age as me, told me that he hadn't performed a backflip in nearly 15 years, then quickly executed a sloppy flip and landed on his feet.

It is frustrating to watch a child try out a new skill like the handstand without hesitation. They have no problem throwing up a handstand, and failing miserably. They shake it off with a laugh and carry on. Our fear is not insurmountable, though. It just takes some planning and strategy, which is an unfortunate circumstance of no longer having a child's brain.

Aside from fear, a second challenge is commitment and consistency. This is often overlooked, yet consistency is paramount in any fitness program. While a lot of trainers seem to embrace the "just do it" attitude, I find this approach woefully inadequate. It just doesn't work. Just wanting to hit a goal does not get it done. Knowing all of the steps does not cause them to magically complete themselves. Deciding to "just do it" may get you started, but it often fizzles out, and the goal is never reached. I am sure you know of someone who desperately needs to quit smoking, but they just can't seem to kick the habit. While the "just do it" mentality works for *some* people, it hardly works for *all* people. In fact, it doesn't even work for *most* people.

Instead, to hit the handstand and any other feat of impressive strength and skill, habit building needs to be built into the routine. You must build an *addiction* that affects your life positively. A good fitness routine should force you to change your daily habits and thought processes. Your goal must be ingrained into the fiber of your day. Building your habits, minutes and days around your dreams and goals is the most important step to achieving them. With that in mind, the handstand must become part of your daily routine starting today - even if only for 5 minutes.

A third challenge is building the necessary strength to hold the handstand position. Without adequate strength, you cannot hold yourself inverted for long enough to learn to balance. Surprisingly, building this level of strength is not difficult for most people. The required strength can usually be attained within 30 days by using only your own bodyweight, even if you aren't in great shape.

Before you can train the skill directly, though, you need to know the fundamental movements. Identifying and learning the fundamentals is *crucial* to your success. After all, you cannot run before you walk, and you cannot walk before you crawl. Similarly, the handstand's key fundamentals need to be identified and learned. For example, is the most fundamental part of the handstand holding a hollow body position with anterior pelvic tilt? Is it adequate shoulder flexibility? Or is it maintaining active shoulders? Maybe, instead, it is to avoid arching your back? It is easy to get confused and focus on the wrong details for months or years. (For interested parties, the most important form elements for beginners are the Cambered Hand Technique, locked elbows and active shoulders. The details are discussed in later chapters).

In summary, you must first focus on building a program that feeds your commitment, keeps you consistent, mitigates fears and builds strength quickly. Once you are committed and strong, your addiction will fuel constant skill work focusing on the important fundamentals.

By the end of this book you should know everything that you need to know about getting your first 15-second hold, along with some information that will get you ready for longer holds and more advanced skills. You should have already read the 15SH progression listed as 6 Challenges in the Chapter 1, which enables you to *start immediately*. The rest of the details in this book are to illuminate the science behind why this system works, and can be read as you go through the program.

The Psychology of Progress

Conquering Fear

Most adults develop a fear of being inverted. Flipping of any kind is seen as dangerous, and handstands are avoided. Our brains turn off to the idea of being upside down. If we take just a few minutes to examine these fears though, you can logically see that these fears are ridiculous. After all, what is the worst that can happen when performing a handstand? If you flip head-over-heels and land flat on your back, is that really so horrible?

Granted, you can land the wrong way. If you are really unlucky (one in a thousand, maybe) you may sprain something when you fall over, putting you out of training for a few weeks. Aside from a freak accident, that's really the worst that can happen.

Unfortunately, realizing that our fears are ridiculous does not eliminate them. As frustrating as it can be, fear needs to be systematically conquered, one day at a time. For a major fear, like an irrational phobia of spiders, this can take years. The fear of handstands, however, is usually not so dramatic. Most people are scared of the unknown - unknown feelings of being inverted, and unknown consequences of falling head-over-heels. Conquering a fear of the unknown just requires consistent and gradual exposure to your fear. This is a behavior modification technique called *systematic desensitization*, and it is built into the 15SH progression in the first section of this book.

Systematic desensitization is only useful if you practice it frequently and consistently. In order to maintain consistency to the program, the 15SH progression uses a 28-day commitment log. In the 15SH program, your log cannot be updated (and thus, your day cannot be complete) unless you have done at least 5 minutes of handstand work. This technique establishes a *streak mentality, which is* a psychological trick to keep you committed to a new habit.

The streak mentality technique is frequently used by successful people who are trying to establish new, positive habits. Jerry Seinfeld, for example, used streak mentality when writing his famous sitcom *Seinfeld* in the 1990's. He would set up a big calendar on his wall, and when he finished his writing for the day, he would put a big X on that day's box. The technique is so effective because streaks are hard-wired into our brain's circuitry. If we recognize a streak in our daily lives, we don't like to break it. We like to stay true to our commitments to ourselves and others. We oftentimes just need to be reminded of our streaks and commitments to remain compliant. All of the most successful people I have worked with have used streak mentality (usually in the form of a training log) to stay committed to their program.[2]

You want to make it as easy as possible to keep the streak going, which means that you want to minimize the *activation energy* of your daily tasks. Activation energy is the amount of perceived effort it takes to complete a task. You are naturally more inclined to feel the quick reward of completing an easier task rather than experience the grueling grind of climbing a mountain of work. Tasks that take a significant amount of effort usually get put off to the side all together. In the 15SH program, I minimize the activation energy by using the *baby steps* technique that is promoted by the social psychologist, BJ Fogg of Stanford University.[3]

The baby steps technique involves setting a very easy daily goal with a low activation energy - something that is easy to complete. In the 15SH program, this means committing to only 5-minutes of handstand training a day. By committing to a very small goal, it is easy to take part in that goal every day, making it easy to keep your streak unbroken. By not breaking the streak, you subconsciously want to build upon it, and 5 minutes per day becomes 10-minutes which, in turn, evolves into handstand training regularly throughout the day. This would be similar to Jerry

Seinfeld committing to write for only 5 minutes a day, but the writing session would then turn into an hour once the ice was broken after the first 5 minutes.

You should start your handstand streak today, and keep track of it using a commitment log as shown in Figure 1. You may also want to start a streak log for another habit, like reading 5 pages of this book every day. Don't delay in getting started -- you should always start when you feel the wave of motivation, else it will wane.

Finally, the last string in our bow in the war on fear is the use of a *safety net*. The nature of the handstand allows for a safety maneuver that changes the worst case scenario from pain (falling head over heels) to safety (returning back to your feet safely). This maneuver is called the *Pirouette Bail*. Once you learn this safety maneuver, fear melts away since you *know* that you cannot get hurt so long as you use this maneuver.

These key components (*systematic desensitization, streak mentality, baby steps* and the *Pirouette Bail*) work together, forming a well orchestrated plan that shatters fear and conquers commitment. Using the 15SH progression, you can quickly overcome your handstand fears while simultaneously building the skills for a freestanding handstand.

The Physics of Balance

It's easy to ignore how complicated it is to balance on our feet. If you put someone under anesthesia and try to balance them in a standing position, it is impossible. Standing tall requires a significant amount of coordination and muscle activation to occur with split second accuracy. We forget the awesomeness of this feat all too easily.

Because we don't think about balance, most of us don't even know how to discuss balance, nor can we identify what balance entails. To discuss balance, then, it is necessary to introduce the basic physics of balance and the terms that describe it.

In the upcoming section, I don't wish to confound you with scientific terms, but aim to give you a deeper insight into how the handstand works. Even though I have a degree in Engineering, Physics was always my worst subject until I was able to put physics into the context of the human body. In the scheme of things, these details are not important if you just want to *perform* handstands. This section is valuable, however, to anyone who is sincerely interested in learning the science of balance and controlling their body in space.

How Balance Works

When trying to balance a tall object on a single point, such as your body on your feet or hands, the goal is to keep the *center of mass (CoM)* directly over a *base of support*. The center of mass is a single point on an object where the weight on either side of that point is equal. So, if we were to place a base of support under an object's center of mass, it would stay perfectly balanced. If we were to place a base of support anywhere else under the object, it would not stay in balance, and topple over. An example of this is shown as a simple see-saw in Figure 23.

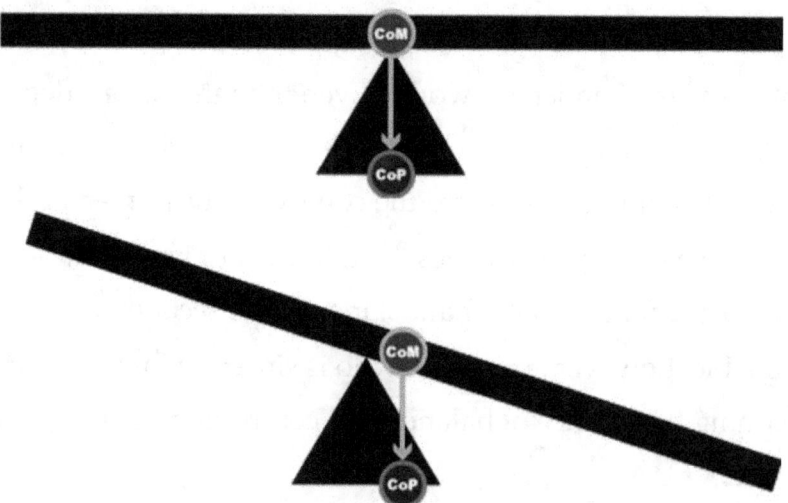

Figure 23: Center of Mass must be over the base of support for balance

Once we know an object's center of mass, Figure 23 shows that we can draw a straight line down from the center of mass through the base of support, to the ground. In order to stay balanced, there *must* be a base of support where that line meets the ground. The point at which the base of support meets the surface of the earth is called the *center of pressure (CoP)*. This applies to all objects, in any configuration, as shown in Figure 24.

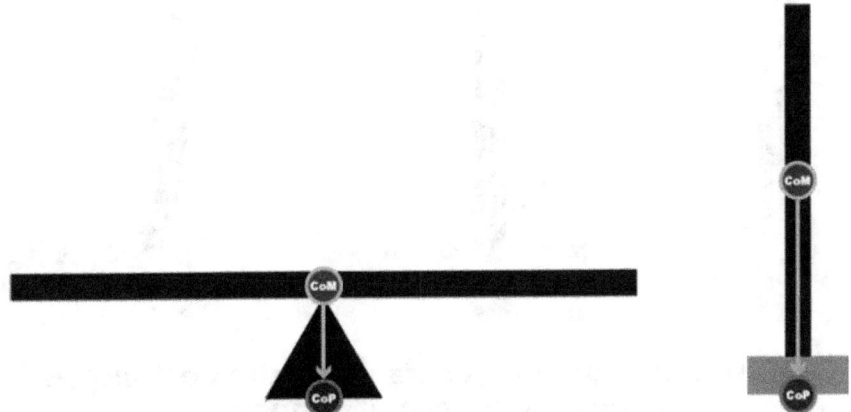

Figure 24: The CoM & CoP relationship compared to an object on it's end

If there is no base of support under the center of mass, then a center of pressure *cannot* be established. This means that the object will topple over until a base of support can be established, as shown in Figure 25.

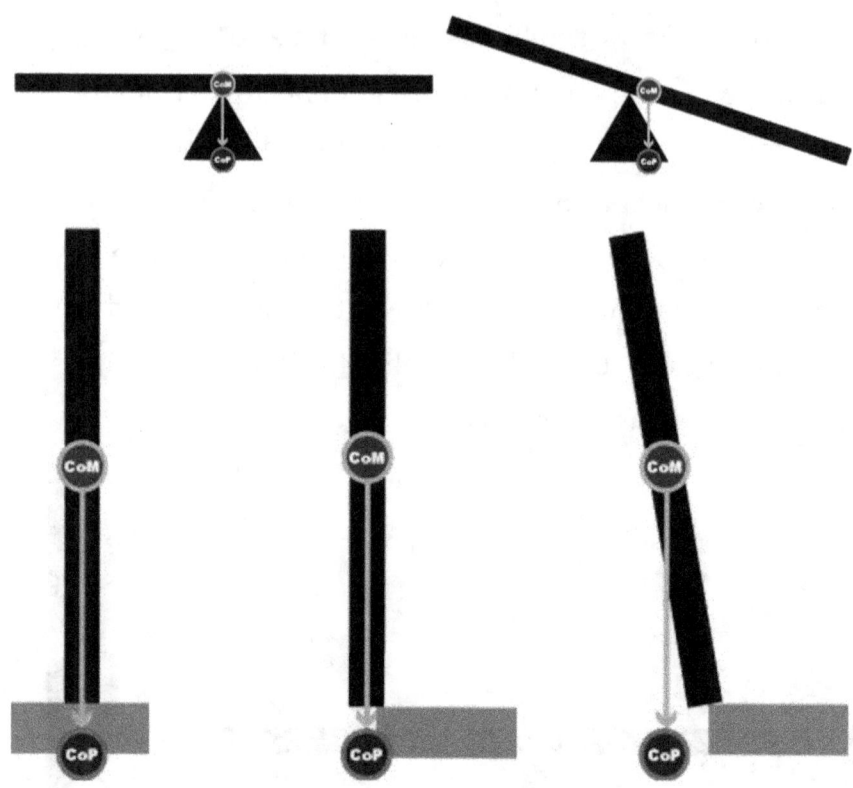

Figure 25: Toppling occurs when the CoM moves beyond a base of support

Translating Basic Physics To The Body

Let's replace our simplistic examples with the human body, standing squarely on the feet. Figure 26 shows someone standing on their two feet in a relaxed position. Notice that the center of mass in the body is around the hips. When standing upright, the center of mass is over the center of the feet, the base of support, thus creating a center of pressure. As you sway slightly from front to back, you can feel the center of pressure change and move around over your feet.

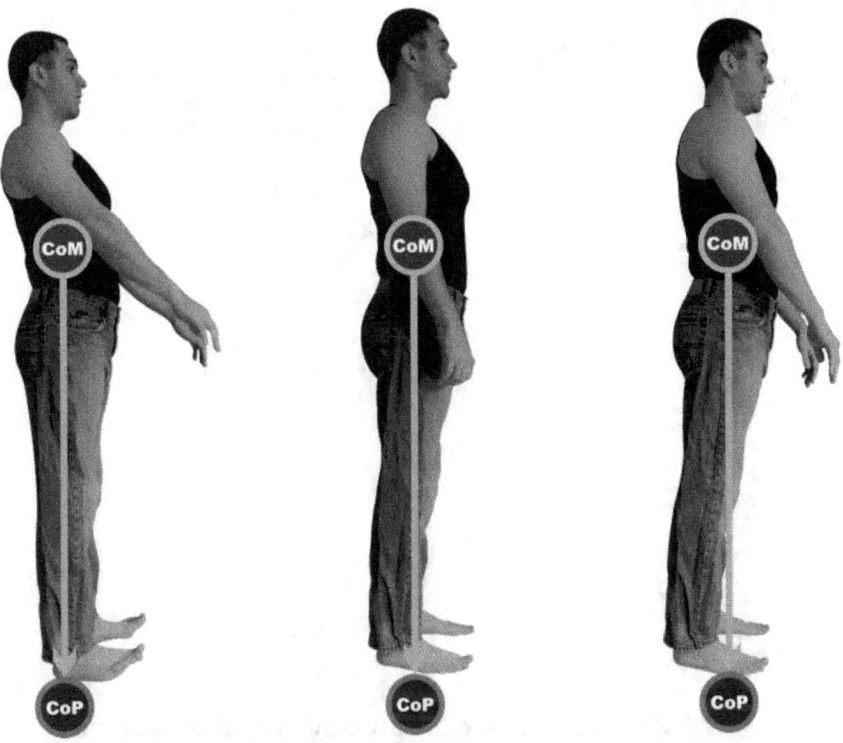

Figure 26: The CoP moves around the foot as the body moves

If your center of mass, however, moves beyond your base of support, you cannot establish a center of pressure. This is when you stumble, because your body instinctively shoots out a leg to save yourself from falling over. Figure 27 shows the situation where the center of mass moves beyond the center of pressure, and the body starts to fall.

Figure 27: Center of Mass beyond the base of support causes a stumble

To fully grasp this concept, try it for yourself. Stand barefoot on your floor. Wiggle your toes. Feel the pressure on your feet. If you are standing straight and tall, your center of pressure is directly below your feet. The arch of your foot (assuming that you aren't flatfooted) is bearing the load, so you feel the pressure on both the balls of your feet and your heels.

Lean back slightly. You should feel the center of pressure shifting back towards the heels. Continue to lean back to the point *just before* you stumble backwards - you should be standing on your heels. Notice how much you have to rock back and forth to stay upright. Your heels start to dig into the ground, trying to push you forward back onto your toes. You may even try to *pike* (bend at the hips) to bring your shoulders over the legs. This is the body's automatic way of shifting your center of mass back over your feet, the base of support.

Go back to standing normally. Feel how your weight is right in the middle of your feet. Your arches put some of the load on your heels and toes, and your toes press into the ground to keep you from falling forward. Now, lean forward over your toes. Notice that the toes squeeze into the ground firmly, keeping your body in balance. Squeeze harder with your toes; the harder you squeeze, the easier it is it pull your body back into proper balance.

These dynamics are incredibly similar to those of the handstand. We want our hands to be as efficient as our feet in correcting our balance. Therefore, you must learn to use the Cambered Hand Technique so that your hands assume a similar shape to the foot. That way, they can use the same mechanism for control.

Cambered Hand Technique

To mimic the shape of the foot and its natural arches, you must practice the *Cambered Hand Technique*. In a nutshell, this technique, shown in <u>Figure 28</u>, puts your hands into a C-Shape rather leaving them lying flat.

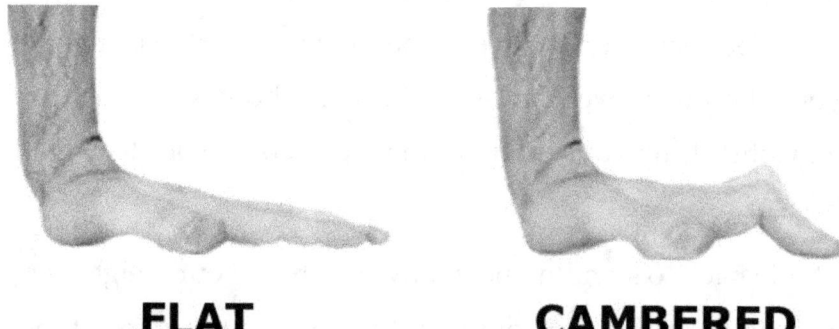

FLAT   **CAMBERED**

Figure 28: Flat hand vs. cambered hand

The easiest way to perform the Cambered Hand Technique is to place your hand flat on the floor, then curl your fingers up so that you can see their underbelly. When you lean your weight onto cambered hands, it should feel quite different from a flat-handed position.

The Cambered Hand Technique distributes the weight between the fingers and the heels of the palms, as well as providing slack in the muscles, tendons and fascia in the forearms and wrists. Aside from providing the benefits of copying the foot's biomechanics, the *Cambered Hand Technique* also significantly reduces the stretch on the finger's flexor muscles on the underbelly of the forearm. This can alleviate wrist pain that crops up for some newcomers.

As you compare the flat-handed position to the Cambered Hand Technique, think back to the example of standing firmly on your two feet. The center of pressure moves around the hands in the exact same way that it moves around the feet. Recall that as you lean your weight forward over your toes, you can feel them grip the ground, helping to force you back and maintain balance. When the center of mass shifts forward, this is called *overbalancing,* and the fingers must squeeze tightly to regain balance. This squeeze pulls the center of pressure back towards the palms, just like the toes squeeze hard to pull you back towards your heels. If the center of mass travels too far over the fingers, the center of pressure moves beyond the base of support, and you need to bail, or topple over.

Figure 29: An overbalanced, but solid/recoverable handstand hold on the left compared to an unrecoverable position on the right, requiring a bail.

Similarly, when the center of mass shifts backward over the palms, the center of pressure also moves over the palms and you are *underbalancing*. To regain balance, the palms press hard into the floor, and push the body back towards the middle of the hands to regain balance. In this case, if the center of mass travels too far over the palms, you instinctively bring your legs down and bail out of the handstand.

Figure 30: An underbalanced, but solid/recoverable handstand hold on the left compared to an unrecoverable position on the right, requiring a bail.

In practice, you obviously don't need to remember all of these details. Instead, you want to remember just *two* things:

1. When you are overbalancing (falling towards your back), *push (or grip)* with your fingers.
2. When you are underbalancing (falling towards your stomach), *push into* your palms.

Once you get a hang of this technique, a lot of the handstand mystery disappears. Even if you get lost in the details of center of mass, center of pressure and the base of support, hand balancing should make a lot more sense when you learn the Cambered Hand Technique.

Optimizing Body Position

Those new to handstands think that some magical, perfect body position will unlock effortless balance. Of course, that means that handstand experts cater to these questions the most. Putting such an emphasis on body position is misguided.

I find that many newcomers work hard for months and then finally accomplish their first 3-second hold. Instead of pride and fulfillment, there is often a feeling of defeat because their form wasn't perfect. Their hips weren't straight, or their toes not pointed. They didn't have the right body position, and thus punish themselves, completely detracting from the fact that they just *hit their original goal.*

Your first handstand holds come down to being consistent, overcoming fear and taking control of forward and backward movement with the Cambered Hand Technique. Having your body perfectly aligned and held in "just the right way" is important, but not for complete beginners. Perfect form is what takes your handstand hold from 15 seconds to 60 seconds and beyond - but you need to get to 15 seconds, first.

Another problem with an focusing on body position is that it is easy to get overwhelmed. Consider the following checklist that is widely considered as "proper" handstand body position, from the hands up through to the toes:

1. Shoulder-width Hands
2. Locked Elbows
3. Active Shoulder
4. Head Looking at Hands
5. Fully-extended Thoracic Spine
6. Hollow Body Position
7. Tightly-squeezed Glutes
8. Locked Out Knees

9. Knees Held Together

10. Pointed Toes

Should you expect to get all of these right on the first try? Or even within the first few months? Definitely not. Can you hold your first 15-second handstand without satisfying all of these points? Absolutely.

Knowing vs. Cueing

I recently attended a Yoga class where the instructor was trying to get the class to fix their posture and stand tall. At the front of the room, she instructed us to engage our glutes, activate our pelvic floor and contract our tummies. Sitting at the back of the room, I looked around and saw that no-one really fixed their posture. The students looked around at each other, doing strange things with their bodies - clenching buttcheeks, and curling over themselves as they contracted their abs. The problem is that anatomical and scientific descriptions are learning how to move. Instead, your brain works much better better when it can visualize a movement, rather than an arrangement of body parts.

Achieving body positions through a visualization is called *cueing*. It is a technique used by coaches all over the world, and in countless seminal works on strength training, such as *Starting Strength* by Mark Rippetoe. If you wanted to fix your spinal alignment using cueing, I would instruct you to "puff your chest out" to straighten the lumbar spine, since this engages the spinal erectors and pulls you into proper spinal alignment. It is much easier for your brain to understand how to puff out your chest than it is to conjure up a method of stacking your vertebrae.

Therefore, the handstand program provided in this book, along with the discussions on body position that follow, all include common cues to learn these positions, so that you can more easily adjust your body into the proper position.

Body Position for Beginners

From the checklist for "proper" handstand form, there are only *two* points that are of interest for beginners: *locked elbows* and *active shoulder*. These are the most important points, because they greatly increase the amount of control you have using the Cambered Hand Technique. The rest of the aforementioned body positions can be *completely ignored* until you get your first 60-second wall handstand, and possibly your first 15-second freestanding hold . Again, body position is important, but focusing too much on body position is inappropriate for beginners. Therefore, I have separated the discussion of body position into *Body Position*

For Beginners (covered in this section) and *Advanced Body Position Discussion.*

Rigid Body

Before delving into the details on locked elbows and active shoulders, it is important to discuss the importance of a *rigid body*. Maintaining a rigid body is often underemphasized by beginners, but it maximizes the effect of the Cambered Hand Technique.

Holding a rigid body means flexing every muscle in your body as hard as you can while holding the movement. After you hit your first 15-second hold, achieving your first 60-second hold will be much easier once you learn to keep the hips, toes and knees just as rigid as the elbows and shoulder.

The cue for achieving a rigid body is to constantly think "squeeze everything". This cue will help you squeeze all of your muscles as tightly as you can. It may help to visualize squeezing your muscles one by one, starting from the hands and working to the toes. Those who have mastered long duration handstand holds surely flex every muscle in their body while holding the handstand, from their triceps to the calves.

Laxity or looseness in your body creates a point of instability and unpredictability. Consider, for example, that you are pushing a pencil along a table. It behaves in a relatively predictable way, rolling along rigidly. Compare this to pushing a wet noodle along the same table. The noodle is unpredictable and harder to move.

When the joints and muscles in the body are rigid, the changes caused by squeezes and pushes from the Cambered Hand Technique are more predictable. The brain, able to predict movements more accurately, can better learn how to correct a loss of balance. The end result is a higher degree of body control.

Once a joint or muscle group relaxes, however, uncertainty is introduced into the system. That same small squeeze of the fingers does not cause the same predictable movement that the brain has learned. The brain gets confused, and needs to process this new, conflicting information. As a result, the brain has a difficult time predicting how much it needs to contract your muscles. The whole system starts to break down, and you are forced to bail.

Now, don't get me wrong - it's possible to hold a handstand with lax or lazy form. In fact, your first 15-second hold will likely be fairly loose, and that's fine. But as you progress from beginner to expert, it becomes very clear that handstands with a loose body are not easy, nor are they impressive. Always squeeze your body tight in the handstand, and you will increase your hold duration very quickly.

Locked Elbows

Locked elbows is the most important handstand element of body alignment for beginners, and is most easily achieved with the cue to "push hard into the ground."

Without your elbows locked, force is not transmitted down your arms effectively. In other words, flexing your fingers in the Cambered Hand Technique will not be as effective in pushing your body into the proper position. Additionally, having your elbows bent usually means that your shoulders are in front of your hands, instead of directly over them. If you were to hold a straight body over your hands with bent elbows, you would be incredibly overbalanced. Thus, to maintain balance, your shoulders close so that your straight body is not perpendicular to the floor *or* your back may arch in an attempt to move mass back over your base of support.

Figure 31: The effects of bent elbows on handstand balance.

It is much more difficult to recover from a loss of balance from the bent-elbow positions shown in Figure 31, because the Cambered Hand Technique has lost a significant amount of its effectiveness. For beginners, this means many failed and bailed handstands.

There is also a biomechanical benefit to locked elbows that greatly reduces the stress placed on muscles. The larger bone of the forearm, the *ulna*, has a curved, hook like protrusion called the *olecranon process*. The bone of the upper arm, the *humerus*, has a small hole at the bottom of it, called the *olecranon fossa*. The olecranon process fits snugly into the olecranon fossa when the elbow joint is completely extended, creating a sensation that the elbows are *locked*.

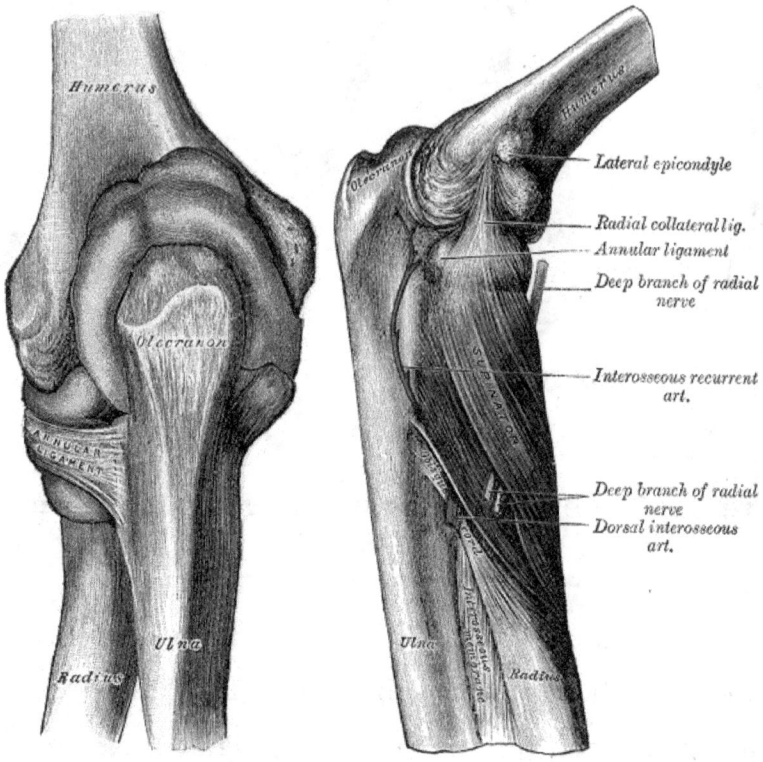

Figure 32: Anatomical drawings of the olecranon process *locking* into the olecranon fossa[4]

The joining of the olecranon process and fossa turns the arm into a rigid structure. The force of the body's load then rests on bony structures, which are designed to bear loads for long durations. If your elbows are lax, however, it is the job of the musculature of the chest and shoulders to bear this load. Bones are much more effective at bearing loads than muscles, so locked elbows means that a longer hold is easier to achieve. Training sessions are also less taxing, letting you practice more frequently.

The only time that breaking locked elbows is advised is when you find yourself woefully underbalanced and need to make a last ditch effort for recovery. Bending the elbows will force the weight of your body to be slightly in front of your hands, forcing your center of mass back over the hands and thus helping you to correct the underbalanced position. Once you recover, you should straighten the elbows again promptly to take advantage of the benefits of locked elbows.

Figure 33: Bending the elbows when you are overbalanced will bring the center of mass back over the base of support.

Active Shoulder

The term *active shoulder* has a different definitions for different movements, but for the handstand, it means to actively and consciously push your shoulders towards your ears as shown in Figure 34. The position is achieved with a cue to "shrug your shoulders to your ears."

Figure 34: Visualization of the active shoulder position.

Here, do this quick test. Grab a broom stick with your two hands and lay flat on the ground on a firm surface. Any floor will do. Now, hold the broomstick and reach your arms up, just like the position they would be in during the handstand. Then, reach way back and try to touch the back of your hands to the floor, while shrugging the shoulders to touch your ears. Go slowly, and don't push it too hard if its tight.

Can you perform this stretch? If you can't do this straight away, you should keep performing this stretch slowly over time so that you can develop the shoulder flexibility required for perfect handstands.

The shoulder is a one of the most complicated and freely moving joints in the whole body, with an extremely wide range of motion unrivaled by any other joint in the body. Holding an active shoulder activates all of the muscles in the shoulder, thus limiting the shoulder to a limited range of motion, keeping it rigid and stable. This simplifies the amount of information the brain needs to process, providing more control.

Compared to a relaxed shoulder, an active shoulder also helps transmit force from the Cambered Hand Technique down through the shoulders. Similar to locking elbows, this means that the small effortless movements in the hands will be amplified and have more impact on correcting balance.

In other words, the active shoulder is <u>absolutely necessary</u> for long duration holds

By focusing on shrugging your shoulders, the active shoulder also opens the shoulder joint. By opening the shoulder, I mean that the arms and the chest appear to be a straight line. It is easier to keep the rest of the body straight when the shoulder is open, but when the shoulder is closed, the center of mass will move beyond the base of support if the rest of the body is straight, as shown in <u>Figure 35</u>. Therefore, a closed shoulder will cause you to either lose balance or need compensation.

<u>Figure 35</u> shows the various ways to compensate for a closed shoulder - none of which are ideal. You can (1) bend the elbows, thus losing the straight and tall handstand, (2) arch the back to bring mass back over the hands, (3) move towards a planche position, by leaning far forward. The planche position is a much more advanced bodyweight skill, requiring a great deal of strength and flexibility, so it is not desirable to try and hit this position as a beginner.

Figure 35: Various states of shoulder position including Open Shoulder; closed requiring compensation; bent arms as compensation; arched back as compensation; and planching as compensation, respectively.

Do note that having an arched back is not necessarily a problem, so if you get your first handstand with an active shoulder and an arched back, it still counts. An arched back is only problematic when you are progressing on to more advanced skills, like 60-second freestanding holds, one armed handstands, and handstand pirouettes. Therefore, if your first handstand is with an arched back you have a right to celebrate, but you should also work on opening the shoulder and straightening the body.

Advanced Body Position Discussion

To avoid over thinking the positions, and thus confounding yourself and hindering progress, I highly recommend that you skip these discussions on the advanced body positions until you can hold a 5- to 10-second freestanding handstand, when they will be of more value to you. If you read this information too early in your progressions, you run a greater risk of over thinking, which is extremely counter productive.

I have listed the notes on advanced body position in order from hands up through to the toes, as I personally find this to be the most effective way to find optimal form.

Hand Placement

For a beginner, the width of the hands does not matter as much - you shoulder really have your hands at whatever distance feels most comfortable. As you progress, though, it is important to experiment with different hand positions that have their own distinct benefits and drawbacks.

For standard handstand work and long duration holds, the hands are optimally placed at shoulder-width with fingers facing straight forward. In this position, the load will be transmitted straight down the boney structures of the shoulder and arms. Any deviation from shoulder-width, and force must be translated laterally, making the move more stressful on the body and ultimately reducing your hold duration.

Placing your hands at shoulder-width is simple, but not intuitive. Most people think that shoulder-width is slightly wider than it is in reality, as shown in <u>Figure 36</u>. Therefore, achieving an actual shoulder-width handstand stance can be cued by placing the hands in a position that feels "too narrow".

Figure 36: Wide hand position compared to a proper, narrower stance

The shoulder-width handstand also translates into many high level skills, such as handstand pushups. In the handstand pushup, for example, arms that deviate from shoulder-width do not allow you push your elbows back. Rather, they flare to the sides, which puts you in a disadvantageous position for balancing during the pushup. The difference is shown in [Figure 37](#).

Figure 37: Flaring elbows can be a problem with a wider stance as you progress to bent arm skills, like freestanding handstand pushups or transitions to elbow levers.

As you progress through to new and different kinds of handstands and skills, you will find that alternative hand positions are usually a big component of advanced skills. In the Japanese Handstand, for example, the arms are spread as far apart as possible as shown in Figure 38. With this hand placement, it is impossible to keep the fingers pointing forward. Therefore, balance cannot come from squeezing the fingers, and must come from pronation and supination (that is, rotation) of the wrists. As a beginner, stick to shoulder-width with fingers forward, and save the alternatives for the days after your first 15-second freestanding hold.

Figure 38: The Japanese handstand is an advanced handstand skill that uses a very wide stance.

Head Placement

I don't stress much on head placement for beginners, because *most* beginners will default to looking directly at the hands. While focusing directly on the hands is not *ideal* it is a lot better than over thinking the movement. Ideally, the head should be placed between the arms, poking out slightly, looking at the hands. You should be able to easily see the hands with the eyes, but arching your head back too far will cause you to overbalance as shown in Figure 39. After all, the average human head is approximately ten pounds, so poking it too far in front of your hands will force you to compensate by arching your back.

NO   YES

Figure 39: Improper head position will pull the center of mass over the fingers, making balance more difficult.

The Capoeira handstand, shown in Figure 40, promotes keeping your head neutral, but I recommend that beginners avoid this position. Firstly, this position makes it much more difficult to fix your eyes on a still object, and requires your head to move quite a bit during the kickup. This sends confusing data to the brain from sensors in the inner ear and eyes, which makes balancing much more difficult (this is discussed in more detail in Chapter 5.) Also, the resulting position requires your form to be nearly perfect, and small errors in form have a huge negative impact on balance. For example, your shoulders should be completely open, which is ideal, but very difficult for beginners, and any arch in the back will cause you to fall over. That is not to say that the Capoeira style handstand is incorrect but it is an advanced skill that takes practice. It should not be on the beginner's path.

Figure 40: Capoeira style handstand with the head in neutral position.

Spinal Alignment

Spinal alignment is one of the most over-diagnosed and over-rated problems in the handstand community. Because the handstand doesn't *look* straight, having an arched back tends to draw a lot of attention when inspecting the handstand. Having an arched back, however, is perfectly fine for most beginning and advanced hand balancers, though.

Ideally, the spine exhibits a straight, aligned posture in the handstand, similar to what is considered good posture when standing. That is, the back maintains a thoracic curvature, and the lumbar spine is arched naturally, without being curved or hyperextended. The similarities between ideal standing posture and ideal handstand posture can be seen in Figure 41.

Figure 41: Standing posture compared to handstand posture

The issue with focusing on spinal alignment is that it is *not important* for achieving a beginner's goal - their first 15-second hold. In fact, many old school strong-men lived and died by the arched-back form of the handstand as shown in Figure 42. The commonly accepted straight back handstand that we see today was only deemed to be the standard by the FIG (Federation Internationale de Gymnastique) within the past 100 years or so. The standard was changed because a straight spine applied better to more advanced skills, such as pirouettes and planches.

Figure 42: Old time strongman performing an arched handstand.

As a result, I tend to ignore an arched back in most new trainees, and don't focus on spinal alignment until they can comfortably and reliably hold a 15-second freestanding handstand. Once you hit that milestone, however, I suggest that you place a high priority on learning the straight back form as shown in [Figure 41](). This is most commonly achieved by using the cue "reach for the sky", where you try to make your body as long and straight as possible, reaching for the sky with your toes. To reiterate, straight spinal alignment will translate into more high level skills, thus making you more capable and impressive in a shorter period of time.

Hip Position

The center of mass of the human body varies from person to person, but it is generally located near the hips. As a result, the position of the hips plays a key role in hand balancing, and in all other bodyweight strength skills. In the handstand, there are four hip positions that are relevant: the arch, the pike, the hollow body, the scissor, and the straddle.

ARCH   PIKE   HOLLOW   SCISSOR   STRADDLE
BODY

Figure 43: The most notable handstand hip positions

Arch

The arched hip position is born out of necessity from having an arched back. When your back is arched, the hip must also arch. Like most beginners, you may struggle to break the habit of arching hip if you achieved your first 15-second hold with an arched back. It is a habit most beginners need to break if they want to progress to more advanced handstand skills. When you are ready to break the habit, you will need to focus on the *hollow body* position, covered later in this chapter.

Pike

In gymnastics and bodyweight skills, the *pike* (or *piking*), is when you bend at the hips. As shown in Figure 44, a full pike is when your knees are just about touching your chest; a half pike is when you make an L-shape.

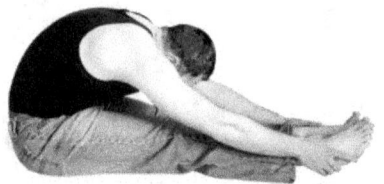

Figure 44: A visualization of the half and full pike

In the handstand, the half pike is used as a display of control. Bringing the legs down into an L-shape shifts your center of mass towards the toes, and thus you need to close the shoulder to hold the position. This is shown in Figure 43, and takes a substantial amount of strength. While impressive, the pike handstand does not actively help you get towards a 15-second handstand hold. It is mentioned here because understanding the definition of "pike" is important for future skill development.

Hollow Body

The hollow body position is necessary for a perfectly aligned, straight handstand. In this position, you actively pull your legs into a *very slight pike* by squeezing your abs. It feels like you are pulling your legs forward, but just a little bit. Learning to hold this position properly makes the difference between your first 15-second freestanding hold and your first 60-second freestanding hold.

Figure 45: The differences between too piked, hollow body and too arched.

As an aside, the hollow body position comes up in nearly every gymnastics move including pushups, handstands, back flips and back levers. It is one of the most crucial skills necessary for all impressive bodyweight strength skills, but is not necessary for your first 15-second handstand hold.

Hollow body rocks, shown in <u>Figure 46</u>, are the most effective exercise that I know for learning the hollow body position. To perform this exercise, lay flat on the ground with your arms extended overhead. Then, use the "squeeze your abs" cue letting your abs lift your legs slightly off the ground. It feels as though your spine should round *very* slightly, and your legs come off the floor. Your body should feel straight and solid. Strengthen this position by rocking your body back and forth for sets and reps.

Figure 46: Hollow body rocks

Scissor

One of the lesser used, but more valuable positions is the *scissor*, where you split your legs so that one leg is in front of the body, and one is behind. The scissor can be valuable to a beginner who is trying to learn balance. Similar to a tight rope walker spreading his arms wide to his sides, splitting the legs in a scissor gives you more control of front-back movement from the hips, as opposed to relying entirely on the Cambered Hand Technique. Also, lowering the legs brings more of your body's mass closer to the hands, thus lowering the center of mass. When the center of mass is closer to the hands, it is easier for the Cambered Hand Technique to move the body in space. Therefore, if you get caught in a sticking point learning handstand balance, you may want to try a scissor position to get a little bit more control while you gradually work up to a full handstand.

Figure 47: Similarities between the scissor and spreading arms to gain lateral stability during balance.

The scissor position is also useful for advanced trainees, as well as beginners. Indeed, with proper form this position can be challenging, impressive and beautiful. Compare the two figures in <u>Figure 48</u>, for example, where the full split is achieved in the scissor position, resulting in a beautiful handstand, compared to a beginner's scissor, used to learn balance.

Figure 48: The impressive full split handstand compared to the beginner's scissor for learning balance.

Straddle

The straddle position is useful for making handstand balance easier. Like the scissor, it lowers the center of mass, thus making it easier to control your balance with the Cambered Hand Technique. However, the effect is not as great as the scissor position for beginners, so I tend to put off straddle handstands until you can perform your first 15-second hold.

Figure 49: Straddle handstand

Straddling your legs in the handstand can be aesthetically pleasing, but is most useful in lowering the difficulty of advanced skills such the one-armed handstand. It also decreases the difficulty of the handstand presses, the planche and elbow lever skills. As such, it is good to know that the straddle position exists, but its usefulness is not for any of the beginning progressions.

Since straddling your legs makes nearly all advanced bodyweight skills easier it is an integral part of advancing into the most impressive bodyweight skill. Pursuing the full splits, therefore, will make it much easier to achieve a high level of bodyweight strength, and I suggest you seek out a good splits stretching program for the long-term benefits. While straddle stretch training and advanced bodyweight skills are outside of the scope of this book, you may be interested in some resources on the topic: I have personally achieved my straddle splits by taking stretching classes at a local Taekwondo gym and applying information from *Stretching Scientifically* by Thomas Kurz and *Relax Into Stretch* by Pavel Tsatsouline.

Leg Positions

In a beginner's first handstand, the knees should be locked straight like the elbows and held tightly together. The toes should be pointed, and the glutes (butt muscles) should be squeezed tightly. The legs should feel rigid and solid. The best cue for this position is "Reach For the Sky", where you actively try to get your toes to touch the ceiling, stretching your body as straight and long as possible. Most newcomers also benefit from cuing to "lock the knees together," which fixes small leg splaying problems that occur from an unintentional scissoring of the legs. These two cues usually help you hit the ideal position easily.

These points are *not* for purely aesthetic reasons. While pointed toes, for example is not necessary for your first 15-second hold, building up to longer holds requires that the body be as rigid as possible. If your toes are not pointed, then your whole posterior chain (calves, hamstrings and glutes) is not rigid, and thus you lose a substantial amount of control over your body.

It is good to build these habits into your handstand as soon as possible after you get your first 15-second hold. The benefits will translate into many other bodyweight skills where a rigid body makes for easier control, such as one-armed handstands and handstand presses.

Losing Control of Balance

Your hips have travelled slightly over your base of support. Your center of mass moves over your fingers, and you squeeze hard, trying to pull back into a good handstand. No matter how hard you squeeze, you cannot pull your center of pressure back to the middle of your hands. You feel as though you are going to fall over. What now?

As you learn to handstand, you will lose control of balance. We know proper body position, and we know how to use the Cambered Hand Technique to regain balance - but that alone doesn't magically unlock the handstand. There will be *a lot* of failed handstands before you reach your goal.

When in a handstand, if you are irrevocably underbalanced, you will instinctively bend at the hips, and your feet will return safely to the floor. Overbalancing, however, is one of the most terrifying experiences to a beginner. Your amygdala, the nagging fear-center of your brain, is screaming at you that you are going to fall over and that result will be painful. Your subconscious and conscious minds are both at a loss for how to safely resolve this problem. It is necessary, then, to learn how to elegantly bail when you overbalance beyond your control.

In order to understand the right and wrong reactions to irreversible balance, think again about balancing on your feet. First, stand squarely on the floor and lean your weight forward. As you lean forward onto your toes, you should feel them digging into the ground. Now, instead of letting them correct your balance, continue to lean forward. Lean so far forward that your heels lift up off the ground. Keep leaning forward and what happens? You hardly fall flat on your face. Rather, your body automatically stumbles. One leg darts out in front of you, and plants itself on the ground, establishing a solid base of support again, with your Center of Pressure firmly within it. You have regained your balance.

Figure 50: Stumbling moves the CoM over a new base of support.

Handstand Stumbling and Pirouette Bailing

Just like balancing on your feet, you can "stumble" forward on the hands in an attempt to regain your balance. When you are on your hands and overbalance to the point where your center of pressure is no longer within your base of support, one possible option is to lift one arm up and take a small step. Similar to stumbling on your feet, the small step attempts to place your two hands below your center of pressure.

Figure 51: Handstand stumbling is similar to upright stumbling

This is *not* the recommended method of restoring balance. For beginners, it is particularly dangerous to rely on a forward handstand walk to restore balance. The upper limb (elbows and shoulders) are not built the same way as the lower limb (hips and knees). The hips and knees are highly evolved for balance, having bony structure and biomechanics that favor standing upright. When you stumble forward on your legs, the hips and knees are structured to make regaining balance easier. The elbows and shoulders, however, do not have such an elegant design for walking. The entire series of joints is so markedly different that attempting a big handstand stride to save your balance can cause your center of mass to hurl even farther forward, which requires another big step to maintain balance. Beginners often fall into this trap, and frantically try to walk their hands under their center of mass again, resulting in a horrible bail resembling a train wreck.

The *pirouette bail* is a safer way of recovering from a gross overbalance, as it takes advantage of the design and configuration of the upper limbs while bringing your feet safely back to the ground. When you find that you are too overbalanced, where gripping into the ground is no longer helping, you lean all of your weight to one arm - the *planted arm*. As you do this, you free your other arm to "stumble" forward. By leaning the opposite side of your body forward, your body will rotate allowing your feet to return to the ground. Unlike handstand walking, your center of mass never gets *too far* away from your base of support, so you won't wildly flail your hands, trying to reach for the next steps and risk falling over.

Figure 52: The pirouette bail, the best solution to handstand stumbling

Note that the pirouette bail is *not* a full pirouette. In gymnastics, a full pirouette is a quarter turn in one direction, and starts with a slightly different hand placement. Rather, the pirouette bail is just moving your hand slightly forward - only as far forward as it needs to go to allow you to safely bring your legs to the floor. In the pirouette bail, you may find that you rotate 90 degrees in a full quarter turn...or you may find that you don't rotate much at all. Either is fine.

Figure 53 below shows some hands positions which are all perfectly acceptable as the final hand placement in the Pirouette Bail.

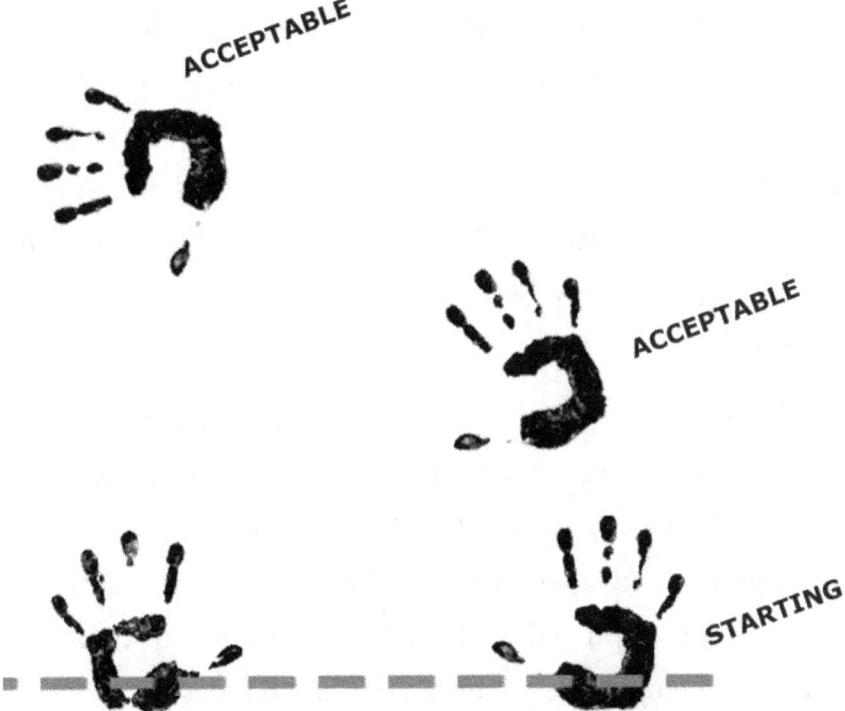

Figure 53: Example of bailing hand placements. You need not turn fully, just enough to bring your legs down safely.

An alternative to the pirouette bail is the *handstand roll bail*, but I mention it only for completeness. The handstand roll bail is not the best for adult beginners learning on their own. It is a relatively technical maneuver, and can be difficult to learn from a book (or even from a teacher). The handstand roll bail can actually create even more fear of handstands, which is already the biggest problem faced by adult beginners. If you have a bad handstand roll bail, you can land nastily on your neck or back. Additionally, you can only do the handstand roll bail on soft surfaces in a wide open space, which is hardly suitable for learning on your own and practicing handstands as much as possible. Since consistency is a main driving force in learning the handstand as an adult, it is not ideal to learn a bail that can't be done anywhere.

The *handstand roll*, however, is a gymnastics and tumbling maneuver that can help as you learn full body *control*. For example, *handstand to roll to front flip* combinations are a very common beginner's gymnastics drill. Proprioceptive drills have their place in your training, but not when you are learning your first handstand as a complete novice. Leave learning the handstand roll until you can hold your first handstand for more than 15 seconds.

Bailing vs. Recovering

Once you know how to bail, temptation to take the easy way out will cause you to avoid fighting for balance. Bailing is a great tool to save yourself from falling flat on your back - its a last ditch effort. Real progress comes from struggling to correct your balance by squeezing your body and fingers tightly in an attempt to recover. The key to getting your first solid handstand hold is learning to lose balance, correct the flaw, and ultimately recover.

If your hips have travelled slightly over your base of support and you are squeezing hard, trying to pull back into a good handstand, you don't need to bail just yet. There is one more thing that you, as a beginner, can do before giving up and bailing. You can break form by bending at the elbow. As shown in Figure 54, bending the elbows not only lowers your center of mass (making it easier to manipulate), but also it draws the hips back, returning the center of mass over the hands. Once you feel that you have regained balance, you should fully extend the arms, and run through your handstand cues to fix your form.

Figure 54: Bending your elbows can help to recover from overbalance (and underbalance, coincidentally).

Note well that learning how to recover by bending your elbows is reserved until *after* you have learned how to bail. By first understanding how to bail, you have removed fear. If you fail to regain your balance by bending at the elbow, you know that you can safely get your feet back to the ground by bailing.

The Physiology of Posture

It is easy to perceive the handstand as a relatively static movement. A perfect handstand, after all, is defined by a rigid body and unmoving balance. As evidenced by the Cambered Hand Technique, though, the handstand requires dynamic movement and control. This section moves into the physiological world, exploring how your body, a self correcting organism, works as a well orchestrated machine to control it's position in space. To understand how the body balances, we need to have a better understanding of how the brain receives and processes information relating to balance.

The Brain's Understanding

I grip a bowling ball in my hands and stare down the lane, eyeing the head pin. I need to hit the head pin on the right side to get a strike. I'm having fun, it's my first throw of the game, and have never been more relaxed - my mind is clear. My hands hold the ball in front of my face, eyes fixed on the head pin and, without thinking much about it, I start to walk towards the lane. Automatically, my arm swings back, and then forward again, launching the ball. Everything felt right, the ball is screaming straight down the center of the lane and smashes the head pin. The pins erupt in complete discord. Strike.

I smile and walk back towards the ball-return machine, waiting for my ball to return for my second frame. I am excited about the strike, and think hard about what I did, trying to recreate the experience. My back felt like it was straight, and I think my right leg swept behind my left. As my ball rolls out, I grab it quickly, analyzing my hand position and how many steps I should take in my approach. My footing suddenly doesn't feel secure, but I approach the lane and launch the ball towards the pins, where it slides way off the side and into the gutter. Has something like this ever happened to you?

For simplicity's sake, the brain can be divided into two parts - the advanced brain and the primitive brain. While this is an oversimplification of the truth, it will serve well to illustrate how two successive bowling throws can be radically different. The primitive part of our brain is automatic and unthinking. It controls tasks like breathing automatically, regulating our heart rate and standing upright. It can also be taught to control the movements related to learned skills, like bowling, or handstands.

The newer part of our brain is advanced and thoughtful. It controls things like planning movements, and staying dedicated to a routine. It processes information from your thoughts, and turns them into actions. This is the part of your brain that says, "Hey, I want to do a handstand right now!" and orders the rest of your body to comply.

When I was bowling, my brain already knew everything that needed to be done automatically on my first attempt. My primitive brain took control, and knew exactly what to do. Without being confounded by the nagging thoughts in my advanced brain, my primitive brain was able to perform the task very well. On my second attempt, however, I started thinking about the intricacies, while ignoring the fact that my body already knew *what* needed to be done. In other words, the advanced brain took over. Since it is not efficient in coordinating several joints and muscles, my performance was not nearly as good.

When it comes to balance, the most primitive parts of our brain have been exposed to standing on our feet from a very young age. The muscular contractions that cause you to stand upright on your feet are offloaded from your advanced brain and relegated to the automatic and efficient primitive brain. Indeed, you have never had to think about keeping your center of mass over your feet before - your primitive brain has taken care of the details for you.

Ideally, we would like new skills (like the handstand) to be handled entirely by the primitive brain. It would be perfect if we could relegate all of the intricacies and minor adjustments of body control to our primitive brains, so that we automatically stand on our hands, just as we do when we stand on our feet.

While this sounds complicated, you have probably done it already at some point in your life. I have done so with bowling, and if you can ride a bike, drive a car, throw a baseball or type on a computer, you have already automated your body's behavior, too. Yet, when many adults try to learn a new skill like the handstand, they often suffer from *paralysis by analysis*, defined by conscious thought dominating over automatic behavior. At best, this leads to stagnation.

Teaching Your Primitive Brain

Jeff has never balanced on a slackline before, but he is with a few friends in the park, ready to hop on the line for the first time. This is his first time even seeing a slackline, which looks like a tight rope suspended just a few feet off the ground. A thin piece of strong, flat nylon webbing is suspended between two trees, and he watches his friends take turns balancing on the webbing, walking back and forth, bouncing and wobbling here and there, but standing upright, no less.

Figure 55: Slacklining, similar to tight-rope walking

It's his turn now, and his friends tell him to stand alongside the slackline as two of them move to his sides. He grabs their shoulders, plants one foot on the line and counts to three. He leans all of his weight onto his friends' shoulders and jumps onto the line, swinging wildly. If he was not holding onto his friends, then he would surely fall straight into the ground.

Jeff, like most people in this position, is absolutely terrified. His brain is screaming at him that he is unsafe. He thinks to himself, "How am I ever going to stand upright on this damned thing?" Here is where most people jump off the line and give up - where most people think they aren't "cut out" for balance training.

Persistently, he stands on the line, letting his mind go blank. He focuses on a stationary tree in the distance, and uses his friend's shoulders to stay upright on the line, with his foot still swinging uncontrollably. After a few *seconds*, passively and seemingly miraculously, his foot stops swinging wildly. Feeling a wave of confidence, he leans some more of his weight onto his foot. Immediately, the line goes out of control and swings wildly again as his brain tries to learn how to stabilize his leg under the new load. He clears his mind again, and in a few more seconds, the swinging calms. By repeating this process, Jeff is able to stand up using only slight assistance. After just a few minutes, he is able to keep the line steady under his body. He still has some training to do before he can start standing and walking without assistance, but he can support his full weight now.

Most people don't understand that your brain can, and will, passively learn motor skills all on its own. Your thoughts or insights will frequently *hinder* your brain's ability to passively learn motor skills like handstand balance. In a very real way, the more you know about the handstand, the more you get in your own way. Counter-intuitively, we often perform better with less instruction, and fewer insights (which is why I recommended that you start the handstand program before reading all of these gory details). In order to harness the power of passive learning, it is helpful to understand how the primitive brain works, and thus how it automatically corrects itself.

With regards to balance, the primitive brain operates like an automated computer that is programmed to process inputs from sensors throughout the body. As this input is processed, the brain sends signals to the muscles all over the body. This results in small, imperceivable muscle contractions that keep you upright.

Every muscle in your body is equipped with *muscle spindles* that send information relating to the muscle's length and stretch. Tendons are also equipped with sensors, the *Golgi Tendon Organs*, that provide information about the muscle's force output. In each ear there is a small, fluid filled structure called the *vestibular system* that detects the head's rotational movement and linear acceleration. The skin uses the same sensors associated with your sense of touch to determine where your body is making contact with the ground - the center of pressure. Finally, your eyesight is integrated with all of these signals to determine your body's place in relation to the world around it. The signals from these sensors all feed back to the spinal cord, and ultimately various and multiple parts of the brain. The primitive brain usually gets the information first, where it is processed, then passed off to the advanced brain.

There are two primitive brain areas that work together to keep you balanced - the *reticular formation* and the *cerebellum*. These areas take the sensors' information and send output to the muscles of the head, eyes and body to keep the body upright and coordinated. The reticular formation and cerebellum have evolved over millennia to work together, specializing in coordination, precision and accurate timing of muscle activation when you do things like walk or play the piano.

While Jeff was slacklining, all of his sensors were rattling information off to the brain very quickly, and he has never been in this situation before. The cerebellum and reticular formation had no idea how to take all of the inputs from the muscles, tendons, eyes, ears and skin, and thus the output was crazy and unorganized. This manifests as a crazed, wobbling foot. These parts of our brain are so specialized in learning motor control that it only takes a matter of *seconds* for them to learn how to organize and process this wealth of new information. You can *see* the brain getting smarter as you watch the foot gain control. When Jeff increases the load on the foot, the sensors in the muscles are now sending different signals, so there is another small adjustment period.

To give the brain an optimal learning environment, Jeff looked at a fixed point on the tree in front of him. The signals from your sensors are more easily processed by your brain if the information isn't changing quickly. Looking at the wobbling line or making sudden movements sends many signals to the brain all at once, and the brain doesn't cope well in that situation. That's why Yoga and dance instructors will encourage you to stare at a single point on the wall when you are balancing on one foot, and why staring at the unchanging horizon can subdue sea sickness (which, after all, is the result of your brain not understanding how to process the movements of a boat). Keeping the head and eyes stationary means that the sensors in the eye and vestibular system are not receiving new information, making the brain's job easier. Similarly, moving the body slowly while you learn to balance has the same effect, which is why you see many talented hand balancers move their bodies *very* slowly and deliberately as they change positions.

To put it succinctly, when learning a new skill like the handstand, simply *exposing yourself* to the skill can have a profound effect on your performance. This is counter-intuitive to someone willing to read volumes on handstand form and body position. More research on proper body position, advanced drills or some key trick does not unlock ability, but it does create two problems:

1. You waste time on changing drills/exercises in an attempt to find *the one* that fixes everything
2. You confound the primitive brain with an overabundance of knowledge

Wasting time on excessive drills and not sticking to a single program is relatively easy to fix. Most people, however, don't recognize it as a problem. But why would you perform five different drills a day if you only really need to do one drill really well? With the handstand, you only need to do one very specific drill at a time - one that focuses on eliminating fear, building pre-requisite strength or exposing yourself to balance.

Confusing the primitive brain with too much information is a huge problem for most of the people I have trained, including myself. Even now, you sit reading pages upon pages of how your brain and body works, and how this applies to the handstand. This will bring your attention to problems that you will try to consciously fix during your skill training. This is problematic because your advanced brain can *override* your primitive brain.

When the reticular formation and cerebellum receive the signals from your sensors, so does the thalamus. The thalamus sends this information onto several parts of the advanced brain, such as the m*otor cortex* and s*omatosensory cortex*. These two parts of the brain are responsible for conscious thought of movement and sensation, respectively. The somatosensory cortex lets you *feel* things in your world on a conscious level, and the motor cortex lets you consciously plan and move around the world.

These parts of your advanced brain are connected to your primitive brain, and they *will* shut down automatic function whether you like it or not. For example, you don't always feel your clothes on your skin. Though, as soon as you read that sentence, you started to *think* about it, and your somatosensory cortex lets your conscious mind suddenly *feel* every piece of thread hanging from your shoulders. Similarly, we don't often think about breathing, but forcing breathing on a conscious level will involve the several parts of our motor cortex. Now that you are thinking of breathing, you most likely find that you need to force each breath, thus suppressing automatic breathing.

When learning a new skill, simply having thoughts about what we should or should not be doing will inhibit and confound our primitive brain. What's worse, the advanced brain often thinks it knows better than the primitive brain, and will force muscles to do things that are not part of the pre-scripted, automatic movement. When learning a new skill, you want to minimize the influence of the advanced brain so that your primitive brain can learn the basics quickly. Then, once you have the gist of it down, you use the advanced brain to fix *one or two* things at a time, to avoid overload.

Thus, the fastest way to teach your brain and progress on a new skill is to consciously clear your mind, forget everything you learned and let your automatic, primitive brain take over. This gives real credence to the old Jazz proverb, "Learn everything and then forget it." When you need to fix a nagging problem like arched hips, for example, you focus on *only arched hips* and let your body figure out the other details.

Physiologically Preparing for Handstands

Contrary to popular belief, the handstand does not require that much strength. If you can hold yourself upside down against the wall for 60 seconds, you probably don't even need to read this section. In fact, most people who can hold a 60-second plank are closer to a handstand than they think. Your first 15-second hold, after all, only requires that you can hold locked elbows and an active shoulder while you are inverted. As explained in Chapter 2, most of the time spent training the handstand is *skill training* rather than *strength training*.

This may come as a shock, because the handstand is perceived as such as advanced skill. Once you have the prerequisite strength to perform the handstand, you can train them several times a day with no ill effect. Compare that to strength training, where performing a maximal deadlift ten times a day would normally cause severe overtraining symptoms.

Keeping the elbows locked and shoulders active are both classified as *isometric holds*. If you have your sights on your first handstand and cannot hold locked elbows and an active shoulder while upside-down, then your training should be focused on increasing the amount of time you can hold these positions. That is, it should consist of isometric strength training which is exactly what the 15SH progression in Chapter 1 recommends.

Isometric strength is a bit different to the kind of strength you associate with lifting weights. Lifting weights for sets and reps is *dynamic strength*. The standard biceps curl is an example of dynamic strength. First you first grab the weight and assume a start position, which loads the muscles in a *loading phase*. Then you lower the weight in an *eccentric phase*, where the *prime-movers* (muscles that cause the movement) are lengthened as the weight lowers. This is followed by a *concentric phase* where the prime movers contract, get smaller, and pull the weight back to the starting position. These phases are the exact same in virtually all dynamic strength movements: loading, eccentric, concentric. (There are some exceptions, like the deadlift, but there is no need to delve too deeply into this here.)

Isometric strength training, on the other hand, requires much less movement. Rather, you load the muscles with some weight and hold it there for some period of time. It is the ideal method for training skills that require you stand still and hold a posture, like the handstand or the L-sit.

When you start training an isometric hold, you first need to see how far off you are from your desired goal. In the 15SH outlined in this book, for example, the first goal is a 60-second hold against the wall. To start, I recommend that you try executing the hold as long as possible to get a baseline of your performance. If you can get reasonably close to the wall, and hold that position for 40 seconds or more, then you can continue to practice maximal holds for 1-4 sets per day until you reach 60 seconds.

If, however, you can only stay inverted for about 15-seconds, and then maximal holds may be a bit too much for you to get started. In which case, I would recommend you follow the prileprin tables as originally devised by Steven Low in Overcoming Gravity.[5]

Max hold	Hold Time Range	Sets	Total Range
26s – 33s	16s – 20s	3 – 4	60s – 76s
19s – 25s	12s – 16s	4 – 5	52s – 65s
13s – 18s	9s – 12s	4 – 5	45s – 60s
8s – 12s	6s – 8s	5 – 6	36s – 48s

Figure 56: Prileprin tables for isometric holds, originally devised by the author of Overcoming Gravity, Steven Low

Based on this table, if your maximal hold is 15 seconds then your hold time during workouts should be 9-12 seconds, instead of your maximum of 15 seconds. You should do this for 4-5 sets (or, until you hit a total hold time of 45-60s across all sets).

If you do not have the confidence to assume a completely inverted position straight away, then you need to gradually and progressively approach complete inversion. You cannot avoid it completely by using a barbell to learn to keep the elbows locked and shoulders engaged - barbells are very different to handstands. Avoiding conquering the fear just makes it worse.

To get started, I recommend that you use the standard pushup position as a complete blank-slate, ground-zero starting point. Once you can hold a pushup position for 60 seconds, you put your feet on the wall with your hips slightly over your head as shown in Figure 57, and build up to a 60-second hold. In the next session, you move your hands a little closer to the wall, and your feet higher on the wall, and aim to hold this for 60-seconds. This ties back in to the topic of conquering fear and Systematic Desensitization Chapter 3, as gradual and progressive exposure will help you habituate and overcome fear.

Figure 57: Inclined plank hold, the next step after a 60-second hold in a pushup position

This technique also exploits a subtle isometric strength training trick. Isometric exercises tend to only increase strength in the exact position in which they are held. In other words, a 60-second hold in the pushup position does not translate very well to the handstand position. However, a 60-second hold in the pushup position will increase strength in a *similar position*, such as your hips being elevated just over your head.

Figure 58: Isometric strength is gained in positions *similar* to the position you are training. A pushup position hold will translate to inclined planks.

Over a relatively short period of time (anywhere from 5-20 days), a 60-second pushup position hold can turn into a 60-second wall handstand, so long as you inch your feet up the wall more and more each day. This approach tackles the issue of strength and fear simultaneously, thus reaching the goal of a 15-second hold much faster.

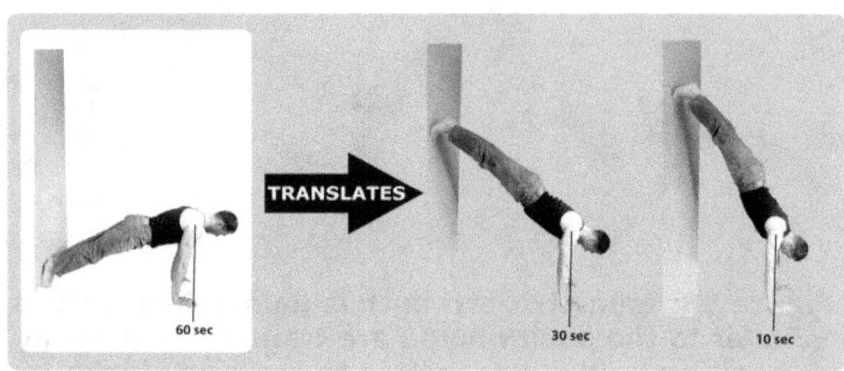

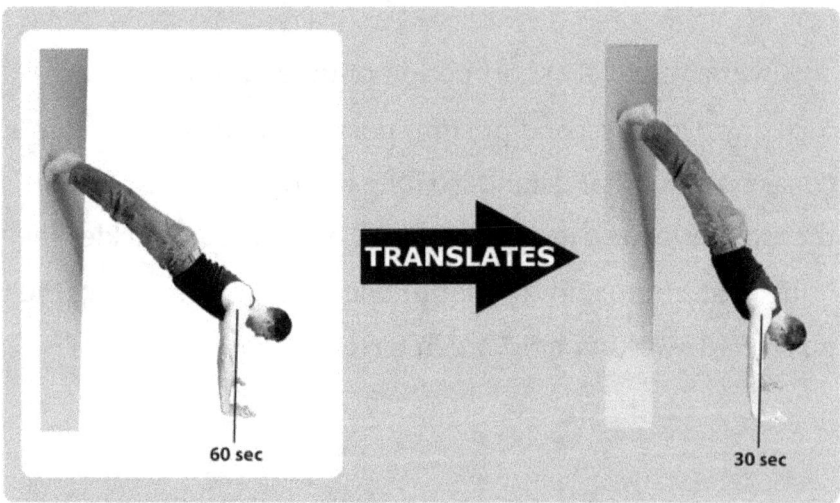

Figure 59: Isometric holds can translate to similar positions, which then can progressively build toward the ultimate goal.

Dynamic Control: The Kickup

These sections on strength and the brain marry nicely with the physics explained in Chapter 4. Controlling your body in the handstand means using your body's natural, passive brain responses to maintain your center of mass over a base of support. Once you are able to support yourself against the wall and bail to safety, the next step is learning freestanding balance. I personally recommend that you use the safety of the wall while you gain control of forward-backward movement using the Cambered Hand Technique. Once you have a good grasp on forward-backward control, you can tackle the first major challenge in dynamic control - the handstand kick-up. The kickup is necessary, because it is the only way that a beginner can achieve a full handstand position away from a wall.

There is a misunderstanding that the goal of the kickup is to move your hips right over the center of the hands, and thus you find perfect, effortless balance immediately. The kickup actually aims to establish a center of pressure over the *fingers*, which is actually slightly overbalanced. Immediately after the kickup, you should have to squeeze your fingers tightly using the Cambered Hand Technique, and pull yourself slightly back to a more comfortable resting position. Then, you begin the dance between overbalancing and underbalancing as the center of pressure moves around under the hands. As you get better at kicking up, you will gain control more easily. The perfect kickup, then, is *slightly* overbalanced, and easily squeezed back into place.

In the earlier parts of this book, I highly recommend only working on one or two things at a time, and harnessing your body's natural ability to passively learn new motor skills. That means I am against flinging yourself into the ground and hoping that the result is a good kickup. Unfortunately, this is where most people think they need to start - but a more effective progression exists.

The technique I employ is called the *Hands Down; Leg Up (HDLU) Technique*. The HDLU technique can be summed up in the following steps:

1. **Hands Down** - Put your hands onto the floor with *cambered hands, locked elbows* and an *active shoulder*.
2. Lean all of your weight onto your hands.
3. Take *one leg* and stretch it as far back as you can.
4. **Leg Up** - Kick your straight leg up over your head *gently* and feel your other leg naturally lift off the floor. Note that the lift from the floor is passive. *This is*

not a jump. Your leg should naturally come off the floor as your other leg goes up. Repeat this process, experimenting with a kick-up that is a *little bit* faster each time until you notice that you can hold yourself up for a second or two.

5. Squeeze into the ground to try and correct the overbalance and stand upright
6. Once your hips are over your head, join your legs together
7.

Figure 60: The HDLU Technique

The HDLU is the ideal starter progression for the handstand kickup. Firstly, it keeps the head and eyes relatively stationary, which, as described in Chapter 5, gives your brain the leg up. Secondly, this progression develops the leg sweeping motion (rather than a jump) to bring the hips over the head. By practicing the leg sweep in the HDLU, you will quickly learn how much power you need in the kick-up. If you sweep the leg with too much force, you will overbalance too quickly, and be unable to recover. If you sweep the leg with too little force, you won't get inverted at all. The HDLU teaches how to kick-up *just enough* to be slightly overbalanced, and also to recover from the overbalance by squeezing the hands in the Cambered Hand Technique.

Starting the HDLU technique against the wall will eliminate the fear of falling over, while allowing your primitive brain to the experience and learn the kick-up. As you get better, and fear dissipates, you must move away from the wall, using the pirouette bail to recover from an overzealous kick-up.

Do note that the HDLU kick-up is not the standard gymnastics kickup. The standard gymnastics kickup has a specific technique that includes a start from a standing position with arms overhead, a forward lunge and completely straight legs throughout the entire movement. This is an appropriate starting place for children, maybe, but the details and technicalities of the typical gymnastics kick-up is needlessly difficult in adult progressions.

As you get better at kicking up, you will eventually find yourself able to progress to a variety of other dynamic control skills. These skills include the standard gymnastics kick-up, handstand walking, handstand pirouettes, and much more. All skills that require dynamic control focus on manipulating your center of mass which forces the center of pressure in new positions and challenging positions. Each new position provides your brain with new information from the sensors all around your body, which will make your handstands more stable and, ultimately, more impressive.

Beyond Your First Hold

While the fastest progress comes when you use this book with the video guides *(available only at chrissalvato.com/ private-video-offer)*, this book should have provided you with everything you need to know about the handstand and getting to your first 15-second hold, at the very least. In fact, most of the information here can easily take you to your first 60-second or even 120-second hold, if that's your goal!

But hand balancing isn't all about long duration holds. It's about learning to control and master your body; it's about doing more with yourself than sets and reps in the gym. And that has great possibilities.

If you've taken the handstand in stride, and are finding that you love this style of training, then I encourage you to do more research. Most people who get their first handstand move on to conquering sports and movements like:

- Pull Ups (my best is +95 lbs. or 159% bodyweight)
- Dips (my best is +135 lbs. or 184% bodyweight)
- Muscle Ups
- Handstand Presses
- Handstand Push Ups
- Handstand Stair Walking

- Advanced Balancing (e.g. Slacklining)
- Gymnastics Tumbling
- One Armed Handstands

And that's just naming a *few!* By tackling the handstand and hitting your 15-second handstand goal, you will unlock a whole new world of sport, movement and athletics. I'm just glad I could welcome you to our ranks.

Stay Strong; Stay Impressive; Keep Training!

Appendix

Pre-Challenge 1: Downward Dog

Goals:
1. Build up to wall planks
2. Get used to inversion
3. Improve shoulder mobility

For some people, jumping right into the inclined wall plank can be difficult. If this is true for you, then hope is not lost, you just need to build some pre-requisite strength first. This just means that your progression may take a bit longer.

People who find difficulty with wall planks usually complain about pressure building up in their head and face, or that they can't stay upside down for so long. To build up to the inclined wall plank, start with the Downward Dog Yoga pose. Downward Dog, shown in Figure 61, is a great pose to ease into handstands because your head is well below the hips, which primes you for being upside down. The pose also requires that you push your head through your shoulders, improving shoulder mobility.

Figure 61: The standard downward dog (left) and another version loading more weight on the hands (right). Both provide a good start to build up to the inclined wall plank.

Daily Routine For This Challenge

5 minutes of Downward Dog practice per day. Attempt at least 1 maximal hold per day, working towards a single hold for 60 seconds or more.

Finer Points

To achieve the Downward Dog pose, start in a normal pushup position and push your hips up into the air. As your hips rise, lower your head through your shoulders. Push your hands into the ground for the entire duration of the hold and shrug your shoulders towards your ears. Once your arms are fully extended, walk your feet closer to your hands, so that more of your weight rests on your hands. You may feel a slight stretch in the shoulders.

Note that you will want to do this on a firm surface where your hands won't slip, like a rubber matted floor or a yoga mat. In this pose, you will also feel a stretch in the back of your legs. This is normal, but not the focus of the Downward Dog for our purposes of learning the handstand.

Once you can hold this for 30 seconds, you may want to retry Inclined Wall Planks (Challenge 1), but some people may need to progress to a 60-second Downward Dog first.

Questions and Answers
Q: My head feels like it is going to explode! What can I do?

A little discomfort of increased pressure is a common sensation for people who are not used to being inverted. If, however, you are experiencing *pain* then **stop the workout immediately** - especially if you notice your eyes going bloodshot. You should check with your doctor, as extreme pain is normally a sign of high blood pressure and, in rare cases, can cause blood to pool in the eyes.

For most people (and those cleared by their doctors), your body simply doesn't know how to cope with being upside down yet, so you need to teach it. To get over this, simply keep practicing and remind yourself to breathe.

Bring your feet up as much as you can, and when your head starts to hurt, take the pressure off by lowering your feet a little. This normally goes away within the first 7 days of consistent training, though it can take up to 14 days, but can sometimes take 6 weeks or more.

Q: I can hold a 60-second Downward Dog, but Inclined Wall Planks are still too hard. What should I do?

If this is not because your head feels like it is going to explode, then you are probably thinking too hard about the Inclined Wall Plank. Really, you don't need to have perfect form on the Inclined Wall Plank. Just get upside down against the wall in any which way. If you are still struggling, contact me directly at handstands@eatmoveimprove.com for advice.

Endnotes

1. From mental power to muscle power - gaining strength by using the mind, Neuropsychologia 2004: http://www.sciencedirect.com/science/article/pii/S0028393203003257
2. *Commit Keeps You Committed To Daily Tasks*, Adam Dachis, lifehacker.com <http://lifehacker.com/5878501/commit-keeps-you-committed-to-daily-tasks>
3. For more information on the baby steps technique, you may be interested on more information by BJ Fogg. There is a great presentation on this topic here: http://www.slideshare.net/captology/3-steps-to-new-habits. While he calls 21 day logs a "myth", I think that Baby Steps and commitment work together beautifully to learn a new habit.
4. These images are taken from *Gray's Anatomy* the timeless (and not copyrightable) text on human gross anatomy. For those incredibly interested in human anatomy, a complete version of *Gray's Anatomy* is available online: http://www.bartleby.com/107/
5. These tables are reproduced with permission from *Overcoming Gravity* by Steven Low. For the most robust and detailed explanation of isometric strength, refer to *Overcoming Gravity*: http://amzn.to/12hUSW7

www.ingramcontent.com/pod-product-compliance
Lightning Source LLC
Chambersburg PA
CBHW070402240426
43661CB00056B/2507